Suad Amiry

SHARON and MY MOTHER-IN-LAW

Ramallah Diaries

Suad Amiry is an architect and the founder and director of RIWAQ, Centre for Architectural Conservation, in Ramallah. She grew up in Amman, Damascus, Beirut, and Cairo, and studied architecture at the American University of Beirut and at the universities of Michigan and Edinburgh. Amiry participated in the 1991–1993 Israeli-Palestinian peace negotiations in Washington, D.C., and from 1994 to 1996 was assistant deputy minister and director general of the Ministry of Culture in Palestine. She is the author of several books on architecture and was awarded Italy's Viareggio-Versilia Prize in 2004 for this book. She lives in Ramallah.

SHARON

and

MY MOTHER-IN-LAW

SHARON
and
MY MOTHER-IN-LAW

Ramallah Diaries

SUAD AMIRY

Anchor Books
A Division of Random House, Inc.
New York

FIRST ANCHOR BOOKS EDITION, SEPTEMBER 2006

Copyright © 2004 by Suad Amiry

The Library of Congress has cataloged the Pantheon edition as follows:
Amiry, Suad.
Sharon and my mother-in-law : Ramallah diaries / Suad Amiry.
p. cm.
1. Amiry, Suad. 2. Palestinian Arabs—West Bank—Râm Allâh.
3. Military Occupation—Social aspects—West Bank— Râm Allâh.
4. Arab-Israeli conflict 1993—Occupied territories.
5. Râm Allâh—Social conditions. I. Title.
DS113.7.A657 2005
956.95'42—dc22
[B]   2005040869

Anchor ISBN-10: 1-4000-9649-9
Anchor ISBN-13: 978-1-4000-9649-7

Book design by Pamela G. Parker

www.anchorbooks.com

Printed in the United States of America
10 9 8 7 6 5 4

In memory of my mother and
for Arwa, 'Anan, Ayman, Diala and Alma

CONTENTS

Contents

Preface

I don't think I ever understood or, for that matter, forgave my parents, or the hundreds of thousands of Palestinians who fled their homes in 1948, until my husband and I had to flee our home in Ramallah on 18 November 2001. The Israeli Army had occupied our neighborhood, al-Irsal, and we had to be evacuated, so we went to stay with our friends, Islah and Saleh, in al-Bireh.

My mother-in-law, who fled her home in Jaffa in 1948, and now lives next to al-Muqata'a (Arafat's headquarters) in Ramallah, told me, "What I experienced here next to Arafat's headquarters was hell; it was as bad as what we experienced in Jaffa in 1948, but this time we knew better: no matter what, you don't flee your town, you stay home. . . . *Ye'ta'hum* (God damn it), there has been nothing but trouble ever since they came."

I decided to take her advice and went back home, only to have to fetch her away from that hell to come and live with us.

Writing my personal war diaries, Part Two of this book, started as a form of therapy during that period, 17 November 2001 to 26 September 2002. Late in the evening, I would often sit down and send e-mails to friends and relatives who were anxious to know what life was like for me during those terrible times. Writing was an attempt to release the tension caused and compounded by Ariel Sharon and my mother-in-law. I hesitantly shared these thoughts with some intimate friends.

It had taken the Israeli invasion of Ramallah for me to realize how incredibly supportive my women friends were (including my mother-in-law, Marie Jabaji). At the beginning my niece, Diala, and my friends Rema Hammami and Vera Nofal read and asked for more, as did my husband, Salim. Later the list got longer, and included Luisa Morgantini, Michal Aviad, Leila Shahid, Penny Johnson, Tania Nasir Tamari, Alma Khasawneh, Vera Tamari, Anita Theorell, Elizabeth Taylor, Rochelle Davis, Marie-Christine Ulas and Taisir Hasbun. It was not until the summer of 2002, when I met the Moroccan writer Fatema Mernissi in Stockholm, that the possibility of publication was raised. It was my women friends again who took action and rushed to publishers with the manuscript. (I had actually lost some of what I had written, and had to retrieve it from friends' in-boxes.) Dafna Golan took it to Babel publishers in Tel Aviv, Luisa Morgantini and Maria Nadotti to Alberto Rollo at Feltrinelli publishers in Milan, Anita Theorell to the Swedish publisher. From then on, Part Two of the English edition of the book *Sharon and My Mother-in-Law* took on a life of its own, a life that I could hardly keep up with. Its relative success encouraged me, seriously and consciously, to start writing what turned out to be my second book (Part One of this book).

The English and American editions bring together what appears in other languages as two separate books and are reorganized chronologically. I enjoyed working with my British editor at Granta, Sara Holloway, who respected my voice, and I am most indebted to my American editor at Pantheon, Shelley Wanger, for her meticulous editing and creative suggestions. Working with her made me overcome "writers' fear of editors." I also want to thank Sahar Qawasmeh for all her administrative help.

The diaries, which span 1981–2004, begin with my journey away from my mother and Amman, the city where I grew up and had lived most of my life till then, to Ramallah, a town under Israeli occupation. The trip, which was meant to be for six months, turned out to be a lifelong journey. In Ramallah, I lived, worked, fell in love, married and acquired a mother-in-law.

The diaries—which include accounts of my everyday life under the Occupation and my frequent encounters with the Israeli "Civil Administrators" and soldiers—took place during major political events that engulfed the Palestinians in the territories during the last decade and a half: the 1982 Israeli invasion of Lebanon; the 1987–1993 Palestinian Uprising, referred to as the First *Intifada;* the first Gulf War, in 1991; the period of relative quiet ushered in by the Oslo Peace Accords (1993); the eruption of the Second *Intifada,* in September 2000; the Israeli military incursion into major cities and towns; and finally the construction of the Separation Wall, beginning in 2003.

It was a dear friend of mine, Bilal Hammad, who taught me once, as we were crossing the unbelievably crowded and chaotic Jordanian-Syrian border, how to step out of the frame and observe the senselessness of the moment. As the years passed, this became a valuable self-defense mechanism against the Israeli occupation of our lives and souls.

Only through taking "one step to the side of life" could I observe and recount the absurdity of my life and the lives of others.

Suad Amiry
March 2005

PART ONE

1

I Was Not in the Mood

Summer 1995

"You kick us out of Jaffa, then wonder how come we're born elsewhere!"

These words flew out of my mouth when I opened it to answer the first in a long list of questions asked by the Israeli security officer at Lod (Tel Aviv) Airport.

I was certainly *not* in the mood.

It was 4:30 in the morning on a hot summer day in 1995. The almost-five-hour flight from London had fatigued me and all I wanted to do was rush out of the airport to meet Ibrahim, who had sweetly come all the way from Ramallah to pick me up at this very early hour.

My anxiety and irritation increased as the young woman at passport control slipped a pink tag into my Palestinian passport. I, of course, have no problems either with pink or with being Palestinian. But at that very moment, all I wanted was a white tag. As I had experienced many times before, pink automatically meant at least an extra hour with security officers at the airport.

Oh, how I wanted a white tag this time!

"How come you were born in Damascus?" the officer repeated, obviously neither pleased nor satisfied with my impulsive reply.

I was not in the mood to tell the security officer that in 1940 my father, who had come to Beirut from Jaffa, was overwhelmed the minute he saw my Damascene mother. She was eighteen, he was thirty-three. He had graduated from the American University of Beirut some twelve years before, while she was still a student at the British Syrian Training College.

The minute he stepped inside the grandiose courtyard of her family mansion in Damascus old town and realized how rich her merchant father was, his dream of marrying this tall, dashingly beautiful woman with greenish-grey eyes started to fade. In the end, this particular dream was fulfilled, but many others were shattered, and my father and mother lived a tormented life together.

I was not in the mood to tell him that in December 1978 my father had died of a heart attack in Prague while attending a writers' conference. The well-known Palestinian writer Emile Habibi was the last person to see my father alive and spend the evening with him.

I was not in the mood to inform the Israeli security officer that every time my mother got pregnant, she went back to Damascus to give birth. In 1943, 1944 and 1949, she traveled between Jerusalem and Damascus to give birth to my sisters, Arwa (a psychologist living in Amman) and 'Anan (a sociologist living in America), and, much later, to my brother, Ayman (a diplomat). She also traveled between Amman and Damascus, where I was born two years after that. I did not want to admit to this, as it would only complicate matters and would certainly increase the security officer's fears for Israel's security, thus prolonging the interrogation.

"Have you ever lived in Damascus?" he asked.

"No," came my brief answer.

I was not in the mood to tell the officer that until the age of eighteen, when I left Amman to study architecture at the American University of Beirut, my workaholic mother, who owned a publishing and printing firm, looked forward to getting rid of her four children every summer. The very first week of our summer vacation, she sent us off to her parents' house in Damascus or to her relatives in Beirut. My brother, Ayman, and I were more than happy to spend part of the summer vacation with our unmarried aunts, Nahida and Suad (for whom I was named), who completely spoiled us and my two teenage sisters. They took us to pick cherries at my Aunt Farizeh's summer house in the Syrian resort town of Zabadani, up in the mountains some twenty-five miles west of Damascus. On Fridays we helped my aunts pack food and watermelons, in preparation for a picnic in one of the many restaurants along the Barada River (which became filled with watermelons that were being chilled), in the lush Damascus neighborhood of Dummar. One of the highlights of our summer vacation was the Damascus International Fair, where Aunt Nahida always bought us what she thought were the latest Russian products: a set of wooden dolls *(matryoshka)* for me, and wooden cars and planes for Ayman. When she ran out of ideas, Aunt Nahida took us for a stroll in the busy Suq el-Hamadiyyeh, where we quenched our thirst with sticky pistachio and gum arabic ice cream from the Bukdash ice-cream parlor. Some forty years later, I can still remember the taste of gum arabic. In the afternoons, while my aunts were having their siesta, we played and ran around the huge water fountain in the middle of the *ed-dyar* (courtyard) with our many cousins. But our summer vacation would not have been complete without a visit to Beirut. After a few days of continuous nagging, my two aunts always agreed to accompany us, or sometimes sent us alone, to stay with Uncle Mamduh and Aunt Firdaus in the neighborhood of Zquaq el-Balat.

To avoid our bad-tempered Uncle Mamduh, we spent most of the day swimming off the crowded St. George's Hotel beach of humid and hot Beirut. At the end of our three-month vacation, and just a day or two before school started, we arrived in Amman and the first thing my mother did was complain about our dark complexions. The Damascenes had an obsession with whiteness, and did not appreciate the concept of a fashionable tan.

"Do you have relatives in Syria?"

"No." End of conversation.

I was not in the mood to tell the security officer at Tel Aviv airport that my mother was the youngest in a family of eleven, and that was just her nuclear family. I did not want to scare him by saying that I had four aunts and four uncles, and more than twenty cousins. They and their families all lived in Damascus.

I was not in the mood to tell the Israeli officer that from 1950 until today, my mother's groceries had been delivered weekly from Damascus. It was impossible to convince my mother that Amman had good meat, vegetables or fruit. This was also the case when she lived in Salt and Jerusalem. The only time she bought local produce was in 1968, when we lived in Cairo. She often complained that the Egyptian Airlines pilots were not as cooperative as the taxi drivers between Damascus and Amman.

I was not in the mood to tell him that Damascus is not, as he seemed to think, just one huge military base filled with SAM-1 and SAM-2 missiles, but rather a vibrant city, especially our neighborhood in the old town where my grandfather's house still stands.

It would have been difficult for me to explain to the Israeli security officer that I have always envied my parents, and even my grandparents, for living at a time when residing in, or traveling between, the beautiful cities of the region was not such a big deal and did not call for security checks. I was always intrigued when my father described his trips between Jaffa and Beirut, which included lunch at a seaside restaurant in Sidon. I was even more intrigued when my mother described to me how in 1926, as a child of four, she had visited her mother's family, the Abdulhadis, in the village of 'Arrabeh in Palestine. I have always been enchanted by the route they took between Damascus and 'Arrabeh, which went down through the Yarmouk valley and the beautiful plains of Marj Ibin 'Amer and Sahel Jenin. "First we went to our relatives in Nablus, and a few days later we went on horses to the village of 'Arrabeh," my mother would say. It was the horse ride which fascinated my mother, whereas it was the very impossibility of taking such a trip between 'Arrabeh and Damascus now which bothered me more.

The security man handed me and my passport over to a security woman sitting in a room behind a desk, then disappeared, leaving me alone with her.

She flipped through my passport, and rather aggressively asked, "And what were you doing in London?"

"I went dancing," I answered, looking her straight in the eye, with an expressionless, tired face, and a voice even more aggressive than hers.

"Do you think you're being funny?" she said, her voice louder and more serious.

"No. And do YOU have any problem with dancing?" My voice was now much lower and more sarcastic.

"What was the purpose of your visit to London?"

"Dancing," I insisted.

As we went back and forth, she started to lose her temper and I started to lose my sleepiness.

A few minutes later, she picked up the phone and started talking in Hebrew, a language I do not understand.

"Dancing . . . Dancing . . . Dancing . . ."—the English word jumped out of her Hebrew sentences.

I was not in the mood to tell the Israeli security woman that I had been on vacation in Scotland with friends, friends I had not seen since 1983, when I had been working on my thesis at the University of Edinburgh.

I did not want to explain to her who these friends were. Going through their names one by one would only complicate matters and make the interrogation unbearably long.

I didn't tell her that my friendships with some of these people went back to the 1970s, and my golden university days in Beirut. Even though I was totally exhausted, I had enough common sense to realize that "Beirut" was a buzzword for the security officers of Israel. Some of those friendships went back to the fifties and sixties, during my childhood and adolescence, growing up in Amman.

As a tall and hugely built male officer (obviously her superior) entered the interrogation room, I was more certain than ever that one should never take the risk of mixing friendship with security issues, especially if it concerns the security of the State of Israel.

As the two officers exchanged a few words in Hebrew, my anxiety increased.

"What were you doing in London?" asked the male officer, extremely aggressively, while looking me straight in the eye.

"Dancing," I insisted.

"You know that failing to cooperate with us on security matters will result in your arrest?"

9

"Fine," I replied, quickly resigned to this ridiculous verdict, "but I need to go out and inform poor Ibrahim, who has been waiting outside the airport for hours to pick me up."

"No, you are not permitted to go; and who is Ibrahim? Is he a relative?"

I did not want to tell the two security officers that Ibrahim was not exactly a relative, as none of my relatives, and neither my husband nor any of my friends from Ramallah, are allowed to come pick me up from the airport. I wondered if the officers knew that I, like many other Palestinians living in the Occupied Territories, needed many types of permits to move about: a permit to enter Jerusalem, another to go out to Jordan, a third to enter Israel, a fourth to work in Israel, an impossible one to enter Gaza, and a four-hour permit to use the airport, which gives you just enough time to get there with no flat tires, *lasamahallah* (God forbid).

Ibrahim is one of two or three taxi drivers in Ramallah who happens to have a car with a yellow license plate, which allows him to pick up passengers from the airport.

I was not exactly in the mood to tell the officer that one of my dreams is simply for my husband to be able to pick me up from the airport or from Allenby Bridge when I come back from a trip. But that is a privilege no Palestinian has.

"You cannot prevent me from going out to tell Ibrahim to leave. It is not fair to make him wait any more, especially now that I am going to be kept here for much longer."

"No, you cannot leave!" screamed the male officer, losing his temper.

"Watch me do it," I said as I turned around and started walking out of the interrogation room into an arrivals hall filled with passengers, many of them coming to enjoy the sun and beautiful, relaxing shores of Israel. My heart was pumping as I walked towards the exit; by then, two security men were walking very close to me, one on each side. One of them kept repeating, "Don't make us do things we don't like doing."

"Yes, arresting me in front of these tourists will create a scene which is not favorable for tourism in Israel!" I screamed back. "Why can't I be treated just like any of these tourists?"

By that time, the three of us were standing outside the arrivals hall, right in front of Ibrahim, the driver.

"*Elhamdullah 'ala es-salameh Suad khir inshallah shoo fi* (Welcome home, Suad, what is the matter, I hope all is well)?" he said as he formally shook my hand, his eyes fixed on the two security officers.

"Where is your luggage?" he added, busy trying to figure out the story of me and the two men in civilian clothes with the hostile faces accompanying me.

"Ibrahim, these are security officers. It is a long story. In short, I am under arrest and I just came out to let you know that you should not wait for me any longer—please call Salim and tell him that I have been arrested at the airport."

"Arrested?" Ibrahim repeated, shocked.

"Don't worry, Ibrahim. It is not a big deal," I reassured him. "I have been arrested because I told them I went dancing in London," I added.

"Dancing? Did you say *dancing*?" Ibrahim was now in total shock.

Oh, God, that was all I needed. It seemed that Ibrahim was even more troubled by my dancing in London than the Israeli security officers. What can I say? I have always believed that the Occupation ruined the spirit of both Israelis and Palestinians.

These were the last words Ibrahim and I exchanged before one of the officers approached Ibrahim and asked him to accompany them. The three anti-dancing men disappeared inside while I stood there outside the airport with no passport and no luggage.

So much for being frivolous, Suad, I started castigating myself.

Less than half an hour later, Ibrahim appeared through the big gates of the arrivals hall, pushing my luggage trolley with one hand and waving my passport in the other. With a victorious expression on his face he said, "Come on, let's go, Suad."

"What happened, Ibrahim? Tell me."

"It takes a man to talk to men," he bragged. "Come on, Suad, let's get out of here. I just assured them that you are a bit strange."

"Ibrahim!" I bellowed.

"But I also told them that you were an important professor at the department of architecture at Birzeit University, and . . . and . . . and . . . and what else did I tell them?"

"Stop it, Ibrahim! *Khalas* (Enough)!" I suddenly realized how much Ibrahim knew about everyone who lived in Ramallah!

Listening to Ramallah's gossip was the only way he could make his daily and nightly shuttles between Ramallah and Tel Aviv airport bearable.

What worried me most was whether Ibrahim had spoiled things for me by assuring the security men at the airport that I had not really been dancing in London.

2

Good-bye, Mother

Autumn 1981

I was crossing the Jordan River for the first time since 1967. This was the start of my grandiose plan to live in Ramallah and work at Birzeit University. That morning, I felt very nervous as I stepped out over the threshold of our house in Amman and asked my mother, "Mama, can you describe to me how to get to our house in Jaffa?"

She sighed and said, "It is going to be extremely difficult, as you have never been to Jaffa, or to the house. You and your brother Ayman were born a few years later."

I must admit I was rather irritated by my mother's remark and somehow insulted, so I retorted, "It is true I have never *physically* been to our house in Jaffa, but I feel I know it so well. Isn't it just next to the train station in al-Manshiyyeh, not very far from Hasan Beik Mosque, and also not far from Suq Iskandar 'Awad? It is just a two-minute walk from the sea. Dad used to walk across the road wearing his swimsuit, his towel hanging over his shoulder. He swam every morning, rain or shine, right? It's the two-story house with a staircase on one side. There are three shops downstairs, one of which is a barber shop. I will definitely recognize it once I see the big lemon tree at the entrance of the house. Isn't the house upstairs ours, and the one downstairs my Aunt Na'meh and Uncle Omar's? Right? Was my grandmother living with us or with Uncle Omar then? When did Grandma die exactly? Of course she died long before 1948. My sisters Arwa and 'Anan were still tiny then, right? Or was 'Anan not even born yet? Anyway, it must be very close to the clock tower—remember Dad telling us how he took the carriage from there when he first went to study at the American University of Beirut in the autumn of 1921. It was his grandfather who accompanied him, as his father had died in an accident when he was very young, Mama, remember . . ." I kept going.

My mother stopped this torrent by saying, "The taxi is here, Suad."

When I looked up, my mother had stiffened. She was staring at me with tears glittering in her greyish eyes. I wasn't sure whether she was crying because I had brought back her pre-1948 Jaffa memories, or because the difficult moment of separation with her youngest child, who was about to cross the river Jordan (which she herself had sworn never to cross as long as there was an Israeli occupation), had finally arrived. Perhaps both.

Oh, God . . . How insensitive I can be sometimes. I should have realized it was bad timing.

Oh, well, I was a nervous wreck anyway.

"Well, Mama, I guess it is time to say good-bye." I was losing my voice.

We kissed. I walked out of the door as quickly as I could. As I was thinking of looking back, I heard her unsteady voice, "Just call Nimir, your father's cousin, and he will take you there."

As the car drove down through the Jordan valley towards the Allenby Bridge, images of 1948 Palestine, which I had collected from my parents' stories over the last thirty years, started flashing through my head. I also remembered images from my own childhood. I remembered the Casino Hotel on the Dead Sea with its exciting little zoo. I fondly remembered Sasha, the monkey we lost as a result of the 1967 War. It was my mother who originally brought Sasha from Beirut. Since we could not find her a proper mate in Amman, she was sent for a honeymoon to the Casino Hotel's zoo. I guess like many other newly married couples at that time, Sasha must have enjoyed the elegant hotel. We used to visit her on Thursday evenings, and spend the night there. I have often been haunted by memories of the reflections of the full moon on the Dead Sea.

Early on Friday morning, my father used to drive us to Jerusalem and take us straight to the Zalatimo sweet shop in the old city. "Remember, this was started by 'Aref's grand-father in 1878, *y'ani* (almost) eighty years ago," my father would say as I was mesmerized by the sight of 'Aref spinning one piece of dough after another in the air. A few minutes later Mtabaq, sweets in round copper trays, soaked in sugar syrup, would be placed on the white marble tables in front of us. As my fingers dipped into the Mtabaq, I tried to figure out how many pieces of dough had flown in the air since 'Aref's grandfather had started this wonderful circus.

"Susu, finish your Mtabaq, otherwise go and wash your hands," my mother's voice would interrupt before I managed to count them. Even now, thirty-seven years later, I still wonder.

Now that fourteen years have passed since I last visited Jerusalem, I am rather embarrassed to admit that it is the Zalatimo sweet shop I remember most vividly of all the landmarks in Jerusalem, or for that matter Palestine. My parents also used to take us to the Hotel Odeh in Ramallah with its tall pine trees and live music, which I never really liked, especially the tango. I guess I was never very romantic.

"Get your passports and permits out for checking."

The driver's instructions ended my daydreaming abruptly. I nervously slipped my hand into my purse and started searching for the permit. I knew I had it, as I had already stared at its Hebrew words several times. I felt extremely uncomfortable carrying a document in Hebrew that allowed me into Palestine. I wondered what it said about me. I wondered if it said that my father was from Jaffa. I hoped it did.

It took me a few minutes to find it; then I handed it with my passport to the Jordanian soldier. I anxiously waited for his reaction. As he handed them back, I sighed and very quickly returned to my daydreaming. I was trying hard to familiarize myself with something unknown and yet also familiar. I felt extremely apprehensive. It was difficult for me to admit that I hardly knew Palestine.

I was sixteen when the 1967 War took place. We never had relatives in the West Bank, though my parents had many close friends there. I was born in Damascus, grew up in Amman and studied in Beirut. All of a sudden I realized that my familiarity with Palestine came only through my parents' recollections and my scattered childhood memories. I remember how delighted I was when my mother, not too long ago, told me that I was conceived in Jerusalem. Oh! How lovely, I thought, especially if the conception had happened after Zalatimo sweets!

I was trying hard to fight my growing fear of becoming a stranger in Palestine. It had all sounded fine when I was trying to convince my mother that my decision to go and live in occupied Palestine was not such a crazy idea.

"It is Palestine, after all," I would often say. That one sentence seemed to have a magical effect on her.

My mother hardly ever lost an argument.

Oh, God, I missed her already.

She never really understood my decision, but I admired her for never trying to convince me otherwise. It simply seemed so crazy to her.

Perhaps I should have let her win this argument as well.

3

Return to Jaffa

I was waiting for the taxi from Ramallah to Birzeit to fill up with other passengers when a rather curious-looking man with greyish hair appeared. He had a big friendly smile on his face and slightly drooping eyes, and as he approached me he said casually, "My name is Salim Tamari. And yours?"

"Suad Amiry." I was a bit taken aback by his relaxed manner, as people had not been particularly friendly since my arrival two days earlier.

"Ah . . . then you must be 'Anan's sister. I was with her and her husband, 'Abdeen, in Boston last week. We went to see a Georgia O'Keeffe exhibition together. I also know your sister Arwa—is she still strikingly beautiful? She was so wild, I had a crush on her, of course, like many other guys at Birzeit at the time. Ah . . . it must have been 1964 . . . or . . . 1965."

What a strange way to start a conversation, I thought to myself.

We both sat in the backseat of the taxi and continued chatting.

"So, it's your first day at Birzeit University?"

"Yes, I just arrived from Amman two days ago."

"How interesting, and where are you staying?"

"In one of the Birzeit University apartments on the Jerusalem road."

"Oh, I know exactly where that is."

"So are you a Tamari from Jaffa?" I asked, though I knew that the Tamaris were from Jaffa.

"Yes," he answered back with Jaffa pride.

"Oh, how exciting," I said, and with a bit of hesitation added: "Perhaps you can help me find our house in Jaffa."

"Yes, certainly."

Later that week Salim and I met at the university cafeteria and decided to venture into Jaffa the following Friday.

I could not figure out whether this was going to be our first date.

In the early-morning hours of Friday, I found myself wide awake, unable to sleep. Going to Jaffa for the first time in my life with such an unusual person would be fascinating. But I was getting very nervous about the whole thing. My brains started to feel like scrambled eggs. "Suad . . . what is it? Is it Salim? Is it Jaffa? Or is it the encounter with your old house?" I started talking out loud to myself, as I stretched out my arm in the dark to switch on the lamp next to my bed.

I burst into tears.

I realized that I was not emotionally ready to make the compromise of going to our house in Jaffa without my father, who had died three years ago. All of a sudden I was so saddened by his death, I felt as if it had just happened. I felt inexplicably angry with him, as if he had let me down. I felt as if I had been totally deserted. I had somehow held on to an image of the two of us strolling in the streets of Jaffa, arm-in-arm, as he pointed things out to me:

"Here is al-'Amiriyyeh school, where Omar and I went," and *"That's exactly where I swam every day, rain or shine."*

And after a long walk, "Here is the cemetery where my father and mother are buried."

My father gazed at me with an almost expressionless face and said, "Suad, just wait for me here, I won't be long," and slowly climbed the flight of stairs that led to our house.

I wiped more tears off my cheeks.

I got out of bed, walked towards the bathroom and looked at my face in the mirror.

Oh, God . . . What will Salim say tomorrow? Will he change his mind about my having the most beautiful eyes he's ever seen? Or did he say they were the most expressive eyes he'd ever seen? If it was the latter, then I don't need to worry. But in any case, I should stop crying, I thought to myself.

I took two ice cubes and went back to bed. The minute I closed my eyes beneath the two ice pads, images from my father's last trip to his house in Jaffa rushed into my head.

I remembered how sick and depressed my father became when he visited his house in 1968. He simply could not take it. It must have been so hard, and now I knew what he meant.

"I was extremely hurt, angry, frustrated, mad, what else can I say, when the Jewish family living in the house did not allow me in. They got so frightened when they saw me on the doorstep of our/their house. They simply shut the door and retreated. They would not respond to my desperate knockings. I was hoping they would open the door once more so I could explain to them that I simply wanted to visit the house, to try to refresh my memories of how things looked. I was curious to see whether any of the furniture was still there. I especially missed my books in the library. I was not intending to take anything from the house. Even if I wanted to do so, I knew very well that they would not allow me. I was not planning to make a scene, as I could not afford it emotionally. During the month before the visit, I had trained myself to restrain my emotions and, more important, my reactions. No normal emotions or reactions were allowed. Everything had to be under extreme control."

At this point, it seemed that my father was mumbling to himself rather than talking to us.

"I thought that the only thing I would allow myself to do, once they let me in the house, was ask for my mother's photograph, if it was still hanging there."

There was a long pause before my father added in a slightly different tone, "Your mother never really liked that photograph. She resented the fact that it was my mother's photo that was hanging over our first marital bed and not hers. I hung it there before we got married and it was rather difficult for me to take it away or replace it."

My father's piercing little eyes were slowly disappearing,

and he sank back in his armchair. His wrinkled dark brown hands hid the lower part of his dazed face.

A minute or two later, with a loud, nervous laugh and tearful eyes, he added, "Anyway, I was saved from your mother's reaction by not being allowed into our house in Jaffa." The story could only have ended on a crazy note, I thought to myself.

He went to bed sick. No one could talk to him for days to come.

Driving my newly acquired little Fiat 127 along the Jerusalem–Tel Aviv road for the first time in my life only added to my already high level of anxiety, which I tried to cover up by being overly chatty.

"Salim, were you born there?" I asked in an attempt to figure out his age.

"Yes, I was two and a half when my parents left Jaffa in 1948."

Only thirty-six! I thought to myself. He certainly looks much older; it must be his grey hair.

I became increasingly apprehensive as we got closer to the clock tower.

And then I got my first-ever glimpse of Jaffa's old town.

OH, GOD, IT'S REALLY SPLENDID!!

A big chill ran through my whole body.

Tears began to run quietly down my cheeks.

I wiped my eyes.

I wondered if we were close to our house in al-Manshiyyeh, but did not dare ask.

Suad, do you really want to go there? I asked myself.

Do you really want to see it?

Do you really want to have an encounter with the Jewish family living there?

Are you emotionally ready for this potentially unbearable encounter?

What if?

What if?

Noticing the state I was in, Salim kept quiet.

Later we stopped at Fakhri Jdai's pharmacy up on Iskandar 'Awad Street. With Salim's distant relative, Fakhri, there was an extremely elegant old man who looked like an English gentleman. He was tall and blond with blue eyes. What was most peculiar about him was the way he dressed: his white linen suit, his thin yellow silk tie, and his black-and-white Clarks shoes (which my father also used to wear), as well as his posture, suddenly threw us back into the British Mandate period. The size of the black ribbon on his white hat was a bit over the top, I thought to myself. He had his hat on, even though it was already late October and he was inside away from the sun.

"Was he left behind because they had to withdraw very quickly?" I wanted to ask Salim.

Soon, we were introduced to him. His name was Signor Allonzo.

"Are you from Jaffa, Signor Allonzo?" I asked in an attempt to end my ongoing fantasy about the whole situation.

"Signor Allonzo is certainly from Jaffa; his family, which

is originally from Italy, has been living here for hundreds of years. Allonzo's family and my family are among the few Jaffa families that stayed behind in 1948. Signor Allonzo is also the honorary consul general of Italy," said Fakhri very matter-of-factly.

Consul general of what country to what state? I was totally confused but of course kept quiet. When my eye caught Salim's, I saw that he was more embarrassed and confused than I was.

It's time to change the subject, I thought to myself, then Salim asked, "Signor Allonzo, do you happen to know where the Amiry family lived?"

"I thought you were a Tamari from al-'Ajami," said Signor Allonzo in a rather peculiar Arabic accent.

"Ya, ya, I am a Tamari," replied Salim, "and our house is just up the hill from here. It is now being used as a recruitment center for the Israeli Army."

"Yes, right," answered Signor Allonzo.

"It is Suad's family house that we are looking for, the Amirys," Salim emphasized.

"Emmm . . . Ahhh . . . Amiry, Amiry."

"Yes, Amiry," I replied with excitement and great hope.

"Is it . . . eaaam . . . is it eaaaa a Muslim family?" he asked a bit stiffly.

"Yes," I answered in a rather low and apologetic voice, for no clear reason.

"Ahhh . . . it must be *tahat tahat . . . tahat* (down, down, there)," he said in a dismissive voice with an even more dismissive hand gesture.

"It is in or close to al-Manshiyyeh, Signor Allonzo?" I asked, trying to salvage a more and more embarrassing and Kafkaesque situation.

"Yes, yes, *tahat tahat,*" he said in the same tone, with the same dismissive gesture.

I was a nervous wreck trying to find out where our house was, and here was Signor Allonzo dressing and behaving as if nothing had changed—as if the British Mandate had never ended in 1948, as if the city hadn't lost most of its Arab inhabitants after the 1948 War, as if the State of Israel had never been created. His prejudices weren't up-to-date either—he was obviously more concerned with my class and religion than helping find our house.

Salim and I looked at one another and thought it was perhaps a good moment to say good-bye.

"It was good meeting you, Signor Allonzo."

"Well, give my regards to Mary and Edmond," he said.

Edmond, Salim's father, had died a few years previously. Salim just nodded and said, "Good-bye, Signor Allonzo."

As we stepped out of the pharmacy, Salim said apologetically, "What a weirdo!"

I looked at him quickly and said, "Never mind, Salim, it was fun."

After a rather long pause, I stopped and looked at him again and said hesitantly, "Salim . . . do you want to know the truth? I really don't want to find our house in Jaffa! I don't think I can take it emotionally. . . ."

I burst into tears.

We walked aimlessly through the streets. I heard people

talking in Hebrew, but I never looked them in the eye. We penetrated the narrow alleys of what was once a flourishing Arab old town and is now an "Israeli artists' colony." How sensitive artists can sometimes be!

A few hours later, we were driving back to Ramallah. The utter silence in the car allowed my thoughts to drift. I found myself reproaching my dead father.

Dad . . . you can't walk out on me just like that, even if you did die. I guess I will never have the courage to visit our house in Jaffa without you.

It has been exactly twenty-four years since my first visit to Jaffa.

The encounter with Signor Allonzo has provided a good story to tell whenever people ask me if I ever visited our house there.

Laughter often ends the story at this point.

4

The Seven-Year Epic of My Identity
1981–1988

I did not care for her.

I was bored.

I invited her to dinner.

It was such a boring dinner.

We had nothing to say to one another.

I proposed.

She accepted.

"We lived together ever after," replied a friend of mine, when I inquired about his wife.

My own marriage proposal was not that different. Perhaps that's why I adored my friend's "tell-it-like-it-is" story.

Autumn 1981

I was madly in love. All I wanted then was to be with him.

He was in Ramallah.

I was in Edinburgh.

It was the phone bills that made his mother suspect we were in love.

Each phone call left me with an unbearable sense of emptiness.

Then the hallucinations started. What if I never make it back to Ramallah? What if the Israeli military governor refuses to give me a permit to visit Ramallah? What if he refuses to give Salim a permit to leave the country and visit me in Edinburgh? What business does a military governor have to interfere in one's love affair?

The mounting longing for my beloved and the ensuing fears and anxieties often made me forget why I came to Edinburgh in the first place.

Oh, God, what will happen to my thesis? How can I write about Palestinian indigenous architecture if I never make it back to Palestine? It's true that *indigenous* means architecture with no architects, but that does not mean a doctorate with no fieldwork.

Oh, God, what a mess this Palestine is!

Spring 1982

It all started in 1982, after the Israeli invasion of Lebanon. I had arrived from Amman to teach at Birzeit University a few months before. I can't say I did much teaching that year, as the university was closed by military order for seven out of the nine months of the academic year. This left me lots of time to fall in love with all sorts of things.

Not long after the invasion the Israeli military governors of Ramallah and Nablus summoned professors from Birzeit and al-Najah universities and gave them the *choice* of either signing an anti-PLO statement or having their work permits removed and being deported from the country.

Deportation meant never returning to Palestine.

I unfortunately belonged to the small category of Diaspora Palestinian professors who did not have a *hawiyyeh* (residency card), which allowed them to live in the Occupied Territories.

I still lose sleep every time I remember those nerve-racking days.

It was like a slaughterhouse. We were all waiting for our turn to be summoned, refuse (it goes without saying) to sign the anti-PLO statement, lose our jobs, and in my case lose a lover, and finally be deported.

One day it was the turn of Professor Mohammad Rashid from Birzeit University, the next Professor Ismail Ali, a few weeks later, Doctor Munther Salah, the president of al-Najah University, and so it went.

Every time I heard about another deportation, I would shudder. I saw my life and dreams breaking up right in front of my eyes.

I tried to think of alternative strategies. I was so much in love that I seriously contemplated the unthinkable: signing the anti-PLO statement.

Why not write to Arafat and explain to him how madly in love I was? I am sure he would understand what love is all about. He must know by now that (strangely enough) I have always been supportive of the PLO. My sister 'Anan is a member of the PLO National Council; in 1970, my father resigned from his job in Jordan in support of the PLO; Arafat must know my family history and understand that my signing of the anti-PLO statement is only tactical. Arafat must realize how crazy and unprincipled lovers (in his case, lovers of Palestine) can be. Everyone knows that Arafat himself was in love more than once. Arafat is the Godfather of tactics. I am sure he will understand.

The hallucinations continued for a few months.

I was not sure why the Israeli governor had not yet summoned me. Perhaps being a woman helped me not to be taken seriously. Perhaps my love story was in one of the Palestinian collaborators' reports and the Israeli governor of Ramallah was now aware of it. One could never predict the weak points of Palestinian collaborators or Israeli occupiers; maybe being in love themselves made them sympathetic to other lovers! You never knew.

As a matter of fact, I was aware that one of our neighborhood collaborators had a soft spot for me. He was fifteen, I was thirty. Love knows no bounds. I like to think that one of the conditions he stipulated when he agreed to collaborate with the Israelis was that they would not deport his beloved neighbor.

I was losing it; Arafat, my neighbor, the Israeli military governor. I wanted to believe they all sympathized with my love story.

Autumn 1982

The decision was made: I should leave the country before I was summoned or deported.

I decided to go away and study for my doctorate in Edinburgh.

Tears ran down my cheeks when the taxi tore me away from Ramallah, away from Salim. He stood there waving farewell as it drove towards the Jordan valley. And I could not help bursting into loud sobs the minute the bus crossed the Jordan River.

I could feel the piercing eyes of the forty passengers in the bus, and the few Israeli and Jordanian soldiers at their respective checkpoints; my crying must have left them with food for thought.

I was totally depressed during my twenty-month stay in Edinburgh. The town's beauty, charm, mystical atmosphere, historic buildings and fascinating Arthur's Seat could not take away my strong yearning for shabby little Ramallah. Scotland's long, dark winter days only added sadness to my misery. I walked for days on end trying to occupy myself with Edinburgh, but occupied Ramallah continued to hold me in captivity.

"Stop crying, Suad, something will eventually work out," Salim's conciliatory, stressed-out voice came through the long-distance call. After some short, some longer, pauses he would say, "I'll give it another try. . . . I'll go and see Eman right away. . . . I'm sure her uncle in Nablus will be able to get you a visitor's permit. . . . If that doesn't work, I'll ask the lawyer to help get you one. . . . I'll also see if Judy can help—I'm sure one of her Israeli friends will be able to pull strings with the military governor. . . . I'll also see the guy in Jerusalem—someone told me if I pay him two hundred dollars he can bribe his way through and get you a visitor's permit."

I was wiping my eyes and my runny nose with the back of my hand when I heard Salim's hesitant words, "If nothing else works, then I will *have to marry* you, Suad."

"Salim, *what* was that . . . ?

"Did you say *marry* me . . . ?

" 'Will *have* to?' "

"Bye, Suad. Talk to you later."

I did not know what to make of Salim's words. I could not help but smile as I recalled my friend's story of his proposal.

My loud laughter and yelps of joy were quickly absorbed by the heavy clouds of Scotland. This did not prevent the shy blue eyes of the Scots from looking at me with sideways glances.

It is true I am not that romantic, but this was a bit much, I thought to myself.

May 1984

Salim was saved, as Eman's uncle managed to get me a one-month visitor's permit from the Israeli governor of Nablus.

I should have realized how far back the Jewish memory can go. If it can go back two thousand years, why can't it go back twenty months?

The anti-PLO statement was waiting for me at the bridge. Oh, how unheroic Palestine and Palestinian lovers can be. Until I wrote down these words, I thought this would remain one of my many undisclosed secrets.

Almost a decade later, when the PLO asked me to be a member of the Middle East Peace Talks in Washington, I realized how pragmatic Arafat was. Or how big my ego was—a member of the PLO delegation in spite of my shameful act.

It was 23 December 1984, six months after my return, and five months after the expiration of my one-month permit, when Salim and I got married. Courageously enough, we decided to cross the bridge and have the wedding in Amman, since it would have been impossible for Eman's uncle to ask the Israeli military governor in Nablus for visitor's permits for all my relatives in Amman, Damascus and Beirut.

We would have a very small wedding party, we thought, since neither one of us could handle a proper wedding scene. As it turned out, Salim could not even handle a small party: he had a terrible flu, and was running a temperature of 102. Every so often the flush-faced groom, who was wearing a suit he had bought some eight years ago for his university graduation, disappeared into my mother's bedroom, then I would go and pull him back out to meet the very few relatives who noticed that the wedding was missing an *'arees* (groom).

Two weeks later, the bride and bridegroom were happily crossing Allenby Bridge together, when an Israeli woman soldier approached, took my one-month visitor's permit—which I had made sure I acquired before I left Ramallah for Amman—and tore it into little pieces in front of my eyes. She coldly ordered me to go back to Amman.

"I am his *wife* now, you can't turn me back. As a wife I have the right to live with my husband," I objected.

My words seemed to have no effect on the soldier's deaf ears. "Let me sign the anti-PLO statement once again," I pleaded, in vain, as neither she nor Salim knew what I was referring to.

There is nothing more frustrating and humiliating than arguing with an Israeli soldier.

Why argue when their minds were made up long ago?

The groom went in one direction.

The bride went back to Amman.

"If the bastards don't give me a residency so I can live with my husband, I will stay 'illegally' for the rest of my life," I told the lawyer friend who had managed after a few weeks to get me another one-month visitor's permit to be with Salim in Ramallah.

No lawyer would advise their client to be "illegal." Realizing the absurdity of the whole situation, he kept quiet.

"Illegal" I became.

Just like the other one hundred and twenty thousand Palestinian wives (with children) living in the Occupied Territories; legally we had rights, but in reality we were "illegal"!

You don't quite get it? Neither did we.

Every time I spotted an Israeli soldier from a distance, I jumped out of the car, turned my back and walked in the opposite direction. If I had been caught with no papers I would be automatically deported out of the country.

This went on for three years.

My poor Birzeit students. I'm not sure they learned much from a teacher on the run.

Summer 1987

Three years later the phone rang.

At the other end was George from the municipality of Ramallah.

"Congratulations, Suad! YOUR NAME IS ON THE LIST OF APPROVED IDS. . . ."

"What?"

My screams of ecstasy almost shattered the crystal champagne glasses inside the dining room cabinet. I frantically drove all around Ramallah and Birzeit looking for Salim. There were parties, dancing, food, drinks, champagne and deafening music. For days on end, neighbors lost sleep as we celebrated my new *hawiyyeh* (residency card).

With Israelis, there is never good news without bad news. All the lucky ones whose names were on the list were instructed to get ready for the big *celebration* with the Israeli military governor and the Israeli-appointed mayor of Ramallah.

And as if it was not bad enough to violate the Palestinian National Movement's call to boycott all meetings (let alone celebrations) with Israeli generals and Israeli-appointed Palestinian mayors, the whole thing was to be televised, on the prime-time seven o'clock Arabic News on Israeli TV.

Salim and I were too embarrassed to reveal the celebration bit to any of our friends, relatives or acquaintances. We just prayed they would not watch the news that night.

The ceremony was to take place two days before the *'Eid al-'Adh,* the Muslim feast of sacrifices. Muslims sacrifice sheep during the *'Eid;* Salim and I sacrificed our political stamina and reputations. All night long, I could hear Salim turning in his bed. I felt sorry for him. I had only brought greater anxiety into his already apprehensive life.

There had been more than seven years of continuous agony over my residency (I would like to think it was over my residency). For the first four out of the seven years, I tried to be legal; this meant long hours of waiting at the military compound every three weeks. It also meant a payment of one hundred dollars a month, almost one-tenth of my Birzeit salary. Every three months I had to go to Amman and wait for weeks before a new permit arrived. It was much easier and cheaper to be illegal for the last three years. Well, easier anyway. I was losing the possibility of a Ph.D. salary at the university as I could not travel to Edinburgh to defend my doctoral thesis. I could hardly remember the topic of my thesis when I finally, three years later, managed to go and defend it during the summer of 1988.

By early morning, Salim and I were getting ready. We changed our clothes several times; by the end, we were dressed in the most boring and subdued colors possible: no red, no orange and no striking yellow.

We both looked miserable in our funereal clothing.

Soon we were among dozens of joyful families in the

military compound of Ramallah. Most of the fortunate ones were peasant women from neighboring villages. The young and happy husbands, accompanied by their not-so-happy mothers, were formally dressed up in their shiny acrylic *'Eid* suits. The wide and colorful loosely knotted ties seemed appropriate for the happy occasion. Some women wore their beautifully embroidered bright peasant dresses, while others had totally covered themselves with long grey or brown *jilbab* dress and head coverings. For a second I suspected that many were deliberately hiding from the TV cameras. Perhaps that's what I should have done.

The happy, "illegal" children, who had accompanied their (so far) illegal mothers, were playing freely on the grounds of the military compound. Watching how unintimidated and free these children were, in the most awkward situation, gave me great hope for Palestine. Occasionally, in passing, the anxious mothers would ask their children to be quiet: "*Khalas yamma, hala' el-jundi bi tukhna* (Stop it, otherwise the Israeli soldier will shoot us)."

Complete silence fell on the assembled group when the Israeli military governor appeared in uniform; a step or two behind him followed the appointed mayor of Ramallah. We all stood up to shake hands.

"This is not the Israeli governor," I heard one old man objecting as he stood up and, with a sweeping movement, wrapped his black Bedouin *'abaiyyeh* (cloak) around his robust body.

"That is Captain Amir," he added.

Neither Salim nor I could tell the difference between the military governor and Captain Amir. But we were somehow relieved. Perhaps we had not completely broken the National Movement boycott after all.

The two boycotted men went around shaking everyone's hands and patting the little ones on the head. It looked more like an election campaign than a residency card celebration. Army TV cameramen followed closely. Salim and I bowed our heads out of respect for the occasion, our chins touching our chests.

Captain Amir stood in front of the crowd and proudly greeted us in his broken Arabic:

"First of all I would like to extend my wishes and the wishes of the Israeli people and government for the holy *'Eid. Kul'am wantu bikheer* (Happy feast)."

"Happy *'Eid* to you," we all answered back, like first graders at elementary school.

"This is a double *'Eid* for all of you here today. This list was submitted to us by the mayor of Ramallah and as a gesture of support for him we have agreed to give you *khawiyyat* (IDs) in the hope there will be more cooperation and collaboration between Arabs and Jews in the future. *Mabghouk* (Congratulations)."

We all clapped enthusiastically. None of us wanted to know what type of *collaboration* the future held for us. Under the Occupation one never knows what kind of price one is going to pay.

Salim and I stood up in the hope that the ceremony was

over. We did not expect the appointed mayor to have anything else to add. As we started moving, the old man with the black cloak stood up to give his written speech.

Captain Amir and the appointed mayor were all ears. They were so attentive and so pleased with his praise particularly of the State of Israel that I suspected they must have written the speech for him.

The cameramen were taking close-ups of the old man's face and then his Bedouin cloak. As the cameramen withdrew, the commanding voice of Captain Amir said, "OK, now the celebration is over. You will get your IDs in the mail."

"What *mail,* Governor?" we all screamed frantically.

"We came a long way to pick up our IDs," said one mother.

"I have been waiting for fourteen years and now you tell us it is in the mail!" came the furious voice of a woman with five little ones hanging on to her embroidered dress.

Fourteen years, I thought to myself! I am lucky. So far it has taken me only *seven* years.

"Not today. Later," came the final godlike words of Captain Amir as he walked away and disappeared into the compound, leaving the appointed mayor to see to his people. The mayor tried his best to assure us that it would only be a matter of a few days before we got our IDs.

How could we believe him when we knew that a letter posted in the post office of Ramallah to another postbox in the same post office took over a month to arrive?

Realizing his helplessness and ours, we all departed.

During this hopeful spell, Salim revived and accepted an old offer to teach at the University of Michigan in Ann

Arbor. I took leave without pay from Birzeit University to accompany him and defend the forgotten doctoral thesis at Edinburgh. We both looked forward to spending a year away from the seven-year epic of my identity card.

But who said it was over?

I told you: with the Israelis, there is no good news without bad news.

On 5 September 1987, Salim left for Ann Arbor all by himself.

On 9 December 1987, the Palestinian uprising, the *intifada*,* broke out. With it ended all Israeli-Palestinian cooperation but not collaboration.

I was all alone, stranded in Ramallah with no ID, no husband, no thesis, no job, no salary and, of course, NO HOPE.

Perhaps it was the newly reversed images of the Palestinians as David and the Israelis as Goliath that gave me the courage I needed for my crazy idea that afternoon.

Or was it that the impossible was now seen as possible and the unthinkable had become reality with the unbreakable will of the new *intifada*?

After seven years I decided to take control of my life.

I could now easily understand how people completely lose it. I could feel the anger mounting slowly inside me. The

---

* During the 1987 popular uprising, known as the First *Intifada,* there was a general civil disobedience movement that resulted in boycotting the Israeli military government, which was called the Civil Administration. It also involved boycotting Israeli products as well a general tax boycott.

seven years of hiding away from the Israelis turned into a strong urge to face them, to look them in the eye and make them realize how criminal their behavior had been towards me and all other Palestinians.

The images of young Palestinian boys and girls facing the strongest military with stones and slings made me feel ashamed of my patience.

I started packing my suitcase: a toothbrush, toothpaste, a towel, a nightgown—no, perhaps pajamas would be better—some underwear, an extra T-shirt, a few novels, a pad of paper, a pencil and pen, slippers, a transistor radio, a few packs of cigarettes.

When I was about to lock the house door behind me, I picked up 'Enabeh (Grapes), my cat, and gave her a hug and a kiss.

"Forgive me, 'Enabeh, I know you're a big girl and can take good care of yourself. I've got to go now." I put her gently on the ground. She meowed back and rubbed her silky body against my shaking leg.

I wept.

"Yes, I have an appointment with Captain Yossi. He just called me and told me to come immediately," I lied through my teeth with a big, friendly smile on my face.

"But Captain Yossi did not inform us he had an appointment," replied one of the Israeli soldiers guarding the huge iron gate of the military compound.

"He probably forgot," I insisted. With all the feigned confidence I could muster, I pushed my way inside the now half-opened gate.

"I have to search your bag."

"Please feel free."

I thought that in itself was a good sign. The two young soldiers were looking through my suitcase. I could see them looking at one another. I could also read what was going on in their dirty little minds. Yes, cooperation between Jews and Arabs, why not!

I did not want to spoil the little act that the two soldiers and I were performing by saying, Captain Yossi, your boss, is my *interrogator*. For years he would summon me, and other professors at Birzeit University. He would put on his unbearably friendly voice, with his distinctive Israeli pronunciation, and call me at my office or even at home: "Suad, this is Captain Yossi from the Civil Administration. Can you come to my office tomoghow at ten in the moghning for a cup of coffee?" The second I heard Captain Yossi's voice I would freeze; I would try to utter a few words, but fail.

"See you tomoghow, Suad."

I would run to the ladies' and throw up.

One of the soldiers accompanied me to Captain Yossi's door.

"Please have a seat. Just wait a little, he is busy with another visitor," came the extremely polite and respectful voice of the soldier.

Never in my life had I met an Israeli soldier with such a normal voice, let alone a polite and respectful one.

It must be my new aura or karma that gave me the courage I needed to carry on with my mission.

I could see that Captain Yossi's secretary did not want to ask too many questions about the purpose of my visit at this odd hour in the late afternoon—all offices dealing with Palestinian permits (work, visit or travel) closed by noon at the latest.

Ignoring the polite and respectful instructions, I walked towards Captain Yossi's door, pushed it wide open and strode forcefully towards his desk.

Taken completely by surprise, Captain Yossi stood up, and so did his Palestinian visitor.

"What is it, Suad? Can you wait outside until I am done with my guest?"

"No more waiting. I have waited for seven years."

It must have been the vicious expression on my face that made the Palestinian man withdraw from Captain Yossi's office immediately. As he carefully closed the door behind him, I could see the secretary's head leaning forward to offer him help. "Get me a cup of coffee and a cigarette," I ordered Captain Yossi as I sat down cross-legged on the chair next to his desk. Not knowing what to make of this reversal in our relationship, Captain Yossi went out and, a few minutes later, came back with a Marlboro cigarette and a cup of muddy Israeli Army coffee.

I never understood how Israelis could drink that terrible coffee. I've been told the army has no time to boil the coffee and the water together, so they just pour warm water over the coffee grains and drink mud. Of course they have no time, as they are harassing us twenty-four hours a day. If they stopped harassing us, they might end up with a better life and a good cup of coffee rather than mud.

Look at the Italians, the Turks and the French: they all have good coffee, now that they have realized it's possible to have a good life without occupying others.

"What can I do for you, Suad?" repeated Captain Yossi with a perplexed expression on his face.

"Give me my *hawiyyeh* (ID)," I said.

"What ID?" he inquired.

"Listen, Captain Yossi, I have been dealing with your nonsense for too long now. Do you have any clue what I have been through in the last seven years, waiting for my stupid *hawiyyeh*? Do you have any idea why every single Palestinian man, woman and child is participating in this uprising? It is because we can no longer take your baloney (a polite word for *shit*). Do you know what it means for a wife to live away from her family, her husband and children? Do you want to know why Palestinian men have been freaking out and running around stabbing Israelis in the back on Jaffa Road? (At that time there were no suicide bombers.) Ask me. I know. I know exactly how it feels to be driven to the edge, of doing mad things. Look at me, Captain Yossi. Do I look like a criminal to you? Tell me." My voice was getting louder with every word.

Yossi was totally stunned. He didn't want to answer yes or no. He did not know what to do with a female professor who was losing it.

"Here—I have packed my suitcase, ready to go to prison after the trial," I added.

45

"What trial?" He was trying to calm me down.

"You claim to be the only democracy in the Middle East. You claim to have courts. Here I am. Put me on trial, charge me for the crimes I have committed (so far). Here is my bag."

I opened it and started pulling things out of it, one item at a time.

"Here is my toothpaste, here are my slippers, here are my books, my T-shirt, my . . . my . . ."

I was taking things out of my suitcase and throwing them all over the floor of his office.

"I am not *leaving*." I stopped for breath and continued. "Put me on trial if you think I am a terrorist. Why not imprison me? You treat us all like terrorists, so we might as well behave like them. Give me my *hawiyyeh*, do you hear me, Captain Yossi?"

I was screaming my head off.

"Seven years waiting for my stupid *hawiyyeh*, does that make you happy? Do you want us to freak out and break down? Look at me. Does that make you happier?"

I burst into tears.

Yossi stood still; like all men he didn't know what to do with a crying woman.

I could see that he was capable of handling Palestinian demonstrators, rebels, stabbers, terrorists. He could handle bombs, dynamite, tanks, fighter planes and submarines. He was trained to handle them all.

BUT NOT A CRYING WOMAN.

NOT A WOMAN FREAKING OUT.

I watched a stunned Yossi walk out of his office. Soon after, he came back with another Marlboro cigarette, another mud (which I drank this time) and a piece of paper with He-brew scribbles on it, which he claimed said, "Give this [crazy] woman her *hawiyyeh*."

Exhausted, I took the piece of paper, walked out of his office and presented it to Captain Rafi.

Captain Rafi looked at the scribbles, looked at me and handed me my *hawiyyeh*.

I grabbed it and walked home clutching it.

I must admit, when I had left home that afternoon, I had no idea what I was up to. Never mind—it worked.

I had 'Enabeh in one hand and my *hawiyyeh* in the other.

"See, 'Enabeh, how they drive us crazy?"

I squeezed her and kissed her again.

Spring 1993

Five years later, the phone rang.

"Hello, Doctor Amiry, this is journalist Yossi speaking. I would like to conduct an interview with you about the last round of Israeli-Palestinian negotiations in Washington for my article in *Ha'aretz*. Can we have an appointment?"

No cup of coffee this time? This was the first thing that came to my mind, but I said nothing.

I could not help but shudder when I heard the voice of journalist Yossi (my interrogator). "Sorry, Captain Yossi. I think this time I am in a position to say NO. You may have changed jobs, become a human rights activist and a freelance journalist, but for me you remain Captain Yossi.

"By the way, I never thanked you for the *hawiyyeh*."

5

The Bold and Not-So-Beautiful

She often passed by the veranda with a huge black garbage bag. From a distance, I would see her energetically swinging it into the already-full garbage Dumpster. The recklessness and joy with which she swung the garbage bags made it feel more like a ball game.

It must have been my long hours of hard work in the soft spring sun, and the piles of books and papers that surrounded me, which gave Um Zahi, my neighbor, the impression that the writing was going so well that I could afford many coffee breaks in her company.

For months on end, I would sit in the glass veranda at the front of our house, laboring through the writing of my doctoral thesis. I had decided it would be best to take unpaid leave, unplug the telephone and imprison myself in total isolation. Having a thesis to write felt like having a monkey on my back. I was trying hard to release its hands and legs, but to no avail.

The burden of my university work and the agony of waiting in line in front of the military compound for days on end to renew my visitor's permits* and, later, to get my residency ID left me with little energy for my neighbors.

It was her little boy Rami, not her, whom I had got to know quite well over the years. Together with his sweet friend, Samir, he would stand outside the low garden wall with his large brown piercing eyes, and watch me mow the lawn. Every now and then, I would call the eleven- and twelve-year-old boys in, and let them dance around with the lawnmower. They enjoyed the dance so much, I would not allow them near the lawn for a few weeks to come.

I never knew what to make of Rami's troubled expression. Unlike sweet little Samir, his face had the agony and restlessness of an old man's. Often when Salim was not around, Rami would appear at the door, holding his book close to his chest, and say, "*Khalto* (Auntie), could you help me with my math?"

The timing was never good, but I helped him for almost three years.

The math book was soon replaced by small presents (which Rami still held close to his chest): a tiny turtle which, twenty years later, I still have in my garden; delicious date

* A visitor's permit, obtained from the Israeli military governor's office in Ramallah, had to be renewed every month for a maximum of three months, after which I had to leave the country for Jordan and apply for a new permit. The issuing of a visitor's permit or the renewal of one often took days of standing in line in front of the Israeli military compound in Ramallah. The *hawiyyeh* is obtained through a scheme called "family reunion," introduced by the Israeli government after the 1967 War to selectively bring together members of separated families.

sweets his mother had baked that same morning; a bright pink and yellow scarf which he bought (or stole from his mother), an electric tableau of Mecca. It was the three red roses that stirred Salim to make a mocking face.

Over the years, math exercises turned out to be the simplest problems to solve in Rami's life.

"Good morning, *jaritna* (neighbor)," Um Zahi would say in a joyful high-pitched tone, often after she had swung the garbage bag.

"Good morning," I would reply in a worn-out thesis-writer's voice, quickly moving my head exaggeratedly back to my notes, as though I was in the laborious process of producing a masterpiece.

Laborious it was.

"Good morning, *jaritna,* how are you today?"

"Good morning, *jaritna,* how are you today? How is your work going?"

"Good morning, *jaritna,* how are you today? How is your work going? Isn't it time for a coffee break?"

Her sentences would get longer and longer by the day until one day I surrendered.

"Why don't *you* come in for a cup of coffee?" I said.

In she came.

The plots of her endless stories would thicken by the day. I was totally mesmerized. Her stories made the writing of my thesis on nineteenth-century Palestinian peasant architecture seem at least one hundred years away.

"You know Khalid?"

"Which Khalid?" I would ask.

"Oh, no! You don't mean *that* Khalid. God, he is so bloody handsome," I said jealously.

"Yes, *that* one," she would say triumphantly.

"He is even younger than my son, Zahi," she would add.

It was difficult for me to figure out whether this was meant as an apology or to show off.

For a long time, I took her stories with a grain of salt.

Lots of salt.

For one reason or another, I always felt sorry for house-wives. Every morning as I drove my car to the university, I would see Um Samir on the balcony hanging out the laundry of her seven little ones, Um Maher taking her two handi-capped sons to sit in her sunny garden, Um Mustafa polish-ing the marble steps of their nouveau riche house. It was only watching Um Sa'ad, who often sat in the shadow of the gi-gantic walnut tree embroidering a beautifully colored dress or destemming thyme leaves, that made me weary of the rhythm if not the meaning of my and Salim's lifestyles, which involved continuous rushing in and out of our house.

I didn't mean to be nosy about Um Zahi's love affair. But she was challenged by the unconvinced expression on my face, and hence instructed me to be on the watch in the late mornings.

Late-morning activities gave me an exciting break away from my thesis.

Every few days I would spot the new blue BMW parked on the main street. From a distance I would see him lock the door of the car and walk casually into the small grocery shop located on the ground floor of Um Zahi's house. It would often be quite a while before he came out with a full shopping bag. He would gracefully walk with the bag up the road, place it in the trunk of his car and drive away.

I was sure some of our other nosy (but not informed) neighbors must have wondered why such a handsome and elegantly dressed young man would carry heavy shopping bags to a car parked so far away.

In addition to running a small grocery shop, Um Zahi was running a spotless home, with seven children (mostly young men by now) and a husband twenty years older. Abu Zahi worked with the Israelis, officially as a civil servant.

Spring 1987

The phone rang. It was Rami.

"*Khalto,* I need to talk to you. Please, can I see you right now?"

"Come," I answered.

His face was pale and even more nervous than usual.

"I am a collaborator," he told me in a reckless voice.

"WHAT?" I shouted, totally unnerved.

"Yes, I work with the Israelis, as a collaborator," he repeated.

Oh, God, what should I say? I gathered my shattered thoughts.

"*Habibi* (dear) Rami, but why?" I felt so scared and sorry for the fifteen-year-old boy.

"I am taking revenge on my classmates," he replied.

"Revenge! Classmates! What's going on here, Rami?"

"I kept asking my friends at school if I could join the Popular Front, but they told me no party would ever accept the son of a collaborator. I told them my father was not a collaborator—he is a civil servant. A collaborating civil servant—he's doubly guilty! they would laugh. They said they would never let me take part in their political activities."

I was still choosing my words when Rami continued:

"You know, when my brother Walid was arrested by the Israeli Army because he was taking photographs near Lod Airport, I went to visit him at 'Asqalan prison. The Israeli captain there told me, 'Your brother is going to get two life sentences.' When he explained what two life sentences meant, I cried, and then the captain said, 'Don't cry. If you work with us we will free your brother in two months.' 'But how can I work with you?' I asked. The Israeli captain told me, 'Just write down for us what goes on in your neighborhood and your school.' When I told him I don't know how to write reports, I always failed in writing at school, he said, 'Never mind, you can speak to me, or when you have news just go and see Captain Rafi in Ramallah. Here are my telephone numbers and Rafi's at home and in the office, and I will ask Captain Rafi to see you in Ramallah.'"

I found myself interrupting Rami: "You have the phone numbers of Israeli officers! And you can call them directly?" I asked.

That is impressive, I thought to myself. That alone would make me collaborate with anyone. Not having to stand in line in the rain and the hot summer sun . . . not having to spend hours trying to get all sorts of permits . . . Rami's voice interrupted my daydreaming, "Yes, I call him whenever I want. Not only that, I go with him to Tel Aviv. On our last visit we had a great time together—he introduced me to some really nice girls."

I did not want to dwell on this angle.

"I also have a bank account at the Israel Discount Bank," Rami added.

I couldn't care less about nice women and a bank account. But that direct phone number blew my mind.

I returned to reality.

"Rami, *habibi,* listen to me carefully. What you're doing is absolutely the worst thing one can ever do in one's life. To collaborate with the enemy, with the occupier, with the one who stole away your land, demolished your people's villages and houses, uprooted olive trees and . . . and . . . Sooner or later the Occupation will go away, but believe me, Rami, a bad reputation never goes away." I wanted to give his father as an example but did not. "*Habibi* Rami, you have a long and good life ahead of you."

"'Good life'?" he repeated after me.

My feelings and thoughts were like a whirlpool.

God, I thought, he is only fifteen.

"The other day I went into the prison with Captain Dani and interrogated the classmates who refused to let me join the Popular Front. I had my head covered with a sack, only my eyes were visible behind two little holes. I pretended to be an Israeli interrogator and faced them with all the details of their lives which I knew from class. They were in total shock, and two of them collapsed and admitted to their acts against the Israelis."

I was speechless. I was afraid for him but also of him. I was angry at him but also for him. God, this boy is risking his friends' lives, but also his own. I wanted to protect him by saving him from himself, from his father, from his mother, from the bloody Israelis, but also from the vengeance of the Palestinian underground.

"Are you disappointed in me?" he asked.

"I will be if you don't stop collaborating with the Israelis."

Easier said than done, I thought.

"Please, *Khalto,* don't tell anyone and I promise you I'll stop seeing Captain Dani and Captain Rafi."

I was not sure who was more naive, Rami or I.

I felt numb for days. The flashbacks of Rami interrogating his classmates did not leave me for months, indeed for years.

And for years I kept my mouth shut.

I wanted to know more about Abu Zahi, Rami's father.

My friends who were active in underground politics told me more than I wanted to know: Rami's father had been collaborating with the Israelis and he often helped the Israeli Army locate wanted Palestinian activists. The shop in front of his house was just a window for spying on our neighborhood. And they told me about Rami's two drug-addict brothers. I thought the story was too much.

Yes, they were in the underground, but I thought their story, too, might need to be taken with a grain of salt.

Until a few months later, when the whole neighborhood was woken by the screams of a mother moaning over the death of her son: Kamal, Rami's brother, had died of an overdose.

I went back to concentrate on my thesis. Nineteenth-century peasant architecture was much easier to handle.

During the 1987 uprising, which lasted for almost six years, I hardly saw Rami, as he spent most of his time away from home in Israel. Many collaborators were killed during that period.

Autumn 1997

Years later, the phone rang. At the other end was Um Zahi, sobbing.

"What is it, Um Zahi? What's happened?" I inquired anxiously as I collected my thoughts.

"Please, please, Suad, come immediately, I badly need your help."

I hung up, rushed out of the veranda door and ran the few hundred feet separating our two houses. I was breathless.

In front of the shop stood Rami and his older brother, Ahmad. They both looked as if they had committed a serious crime, or were about to do so. The rage on their faces alarmed me and made me hesitate.

Once again, I had been sucked into Um Zahi's and Rami's lives.

"Hello, Rami," I said.

No answer.

I suddenly noticed the shattered glass of the shop window behind his back.

"Rami, what happened?" I asked.

Still no answer. Rami and Ahmad exchanged glances, then looked straight at me.

"Is your mother home?" I filled the horrible silence.

"Did she call you?" asked Rami.

"Yes," I answered as I walked past them. I strode along the side of the two-story house and entered the staircase leading up to Um Zahi's apartment.

The door was wide open. In the sitting room, with its huge purple and brown sofas, sat Abu Zahi and a middle-aged, dusty man with grey hair, who pulled his trousers over his dangling stomach as he stood up to shake my hand.

"*Ahlan, ahlan* (Welcome, welcome), Doctor Suad. What a nice surprise!" said Abu Zahi.

"Where is Um Zahi?" I asked at once.

"Right there," he said, pointing to the bedroom immediately off the salon.

As soon as I started to cross the salon diagonally towards Um Zahi's bedroom, I could hear Abu Zahi bargaining again with his visitor about the prices of cement, stone and reinforced steel.

"How much did you say three feet of stone costs?"

"What a pity, we should have added a floor before Oslo. Prices were much cheaper then, but we did not have the money."

"How can it be cheaper when you didn't have the money?" said the contractor, trying to outsmart Abu Zahi.

I wanted to knock, but Um Zahi was standing at her wide-open bedroom door. Her eyes were a bit red but not as bad as I had imagined.

"Tell him I am not a whore," she said.

"What?" I gasped.

"Yes, tell him I am not a whore," she repeated.

My immediate reaction was to enter her room and close the door behind me as fast as I could. (I did not think the contractor's cement and stone prices provided the right backdrop to this story.)

She started sobbing again. I held her hand and sat next to her on the bed.

"Easy, easy, Um Zahi, you're going to be all right," I tried to comfort her.

Oh, my God, I thought, she must have had a terrible fight with her husband. Here he is, coolly bargaining with the contractor, planning to build a new house. It must be for a new wife he is planning to marry. No wonder she is sobbing. Oh, what pigs men can be!

"Rami, the bastard, is accusing me of being a whore," she brought me back to reality.

"A whore? Rami?" I repeated after her, trying hard to grasp the situation.

"Yes, Rami. That's what he told me when I asked him to stop fucking around with Jamileh."

"What? His brother's wife?" I gasped in disbelief.

I must finish chapter three of my thesis, was my immediate reaction.

"Yes, I know it for a fact. He is madly in love with Ahmad's wife, and every time poor Ahmad goes to work in Israel and stays overnight, Rami fucks around with her. And when I confront him with it and ask him to stop, he says to me, 'Mind your own business, whore.'" The sobbing continued.

It was a Palestinian version of *The Bold and the Beautiful.*

I searched for a meaningful response.

"Um Zahi, you call your son a bastard? You tell your son he is fooling around with his sister-in-law? Even if it was right, you should never call your son a bastard." These were the most profound words I could muster.

"My favorite son calls me a whore," she said as she wiped her tears.

"But he is trying to get back at you," I tried to explain.

The sobbing stopped.

"You know what Rami told me?" she said in a rather nostalgic voice. "He said, 'You think I am stupid? Remember twelve years ago when you were fucking around with your beloved Khalid? You thought I was a stupid little boy, didn't you? You think I didn't notice what was going on? Yes, I was only a boy then, but I knew it all, whore. And I kept my mouth shut all these years.'"

See what good training Palestinian collaborators get from Israel?

Rami walked into his mother's bedroom as she was

59

telling me what had happened. The open door behind him distracted me more than his presence. Being an architect made me concentrate more on the prices of concrete and reinforced steel. I must have been worried that the contractor was not giving Abu Zahi a good deal.

"Suad, wasn't my mother fucking around with Khalid some twelve years ago? Wasn't she coming to cry on your shoulder? Didn't you once give her a ride to his house?"

I took a deep breath and with an authoritative aunt's voice said, "Rami, for God's sake, just stop it, stop this nonsense. She is your mother, after all."

"What kind of a mother is she when she accuses me of being in love with my brother's wife?"

I could see tears in Rami's eyes.

"Suad, please don't listen to her." He turned his back and walked away.

I was trying to take an even deeper breath when Abu Zahi appeared at the door. I could not deal with one more character in this soap opera.

"Um Zahi, the contractor needs eight hundred dollars as a down payment. Where is the money?"

"Right there in the cupboard, under the folded shirts," Um Zahi said without sobs, in her normal voice. Abu Zahi walked towards the cupboard.

"All right, there it is," he said as he took the money back to the salon.

"Promise, good-quality stone."

"*Walaw ya Zalameh ahsan hajar* (Of course, man . . . for you the best)."

60

I was still searching for conciliatory words for Um Zahi when her face lit up and in the most joyful tone she told me: "Ah, Suad, I forgot to tell you that Abu Zahi and I are going on the *hajj* this spring. You know they agreed to register our names this year, unlike last year. You know how much the *hajj* costs for each one of us?"

I was hoping the *hajj* cost less than eight hundred dollars, the cost of cement and stone.

"Congratulations, Um Zahi, that is really nice." I was delighted to have the right words for *this* occasion.

Never in my life had I appreciated the *hajj* so much.

As I went back home, the images of the broken shop window, the expressions on Rami's and Ahmad's faces, the whore, the bastard, the prices of the cement and stone, the brother's wife Jamileh, the civil servant, the collaborator, the drug addict, the drug overdose, and finally the image of Um Zahi and Abu Zahi walking around the black stone in Mecca, made me realize how uninteresting my thesis really was, and perhaps my life too.

A few weeks later the glittering red and green lights reading *Hajj Mabrouk* which welcomed Um Zahi and Abu Zahi back from Mecca tempted me to pay them a visit, but this time I exercised self-control.

A few months later, from a distance, I saw Um Zahi walking downtown. She was totally covered with a *jallabiyyeh* and a *hijab*.

6

A Shopping Spree in Anticipation of Saddam's Scud Missiles

February 1991

I stared deep into his eyes.

I had always wanted to do this, but had been too scared.

I could not take my eyes off him.

At first he did not notice me, or perhaps he had decided to ignore me.

Every time he stole a quick glance in my direction, my eyes were on him.

I was trembling inside, in spite of my calm appearance.

I could hear my heart beating.

The more nervous he became, the more satisfied I was.

It was a long-overdue revenge.

It was the third week of the 1991 Gulf War. I had no idea why the Israeli Army had lifted the curfew at this odd time: between 3 and 6 p.m. in the afternoon. They often lifted curfews in the early morning, or by noon at the latest. Maybe the Israeli military commander had had a late date with his woman the night before. Maybe he had forgotten that we were under curfew that day, who knows?

We're never sure how serious or unserious this occupation is.

"Do you want to go out shopping with us?" Salim had asked hesitantly, knowing my answer in advance.

"No, take your mother and go."

"OK," came his quick and resigned reply.

"Why aren't you coming with us?" I heard the inquisitive voice of my mother-in-law, who was getting dressed in her bedroom. She had come to live with us when the war started, and stayed until the curfew was over.

"Aren't you sick and tired of staying home? We've already been stuck under curfew for three weeks now. God knows, it may go on for another three months . . . if not more. *Haram aleiki Suad, ta'ali shimi shwayyet hawa* (Poor thing, come get some fresh air)."

"Are you sure it is fresh air, Um Salim? Perhaps Saddam will send his chemical Scuds this afternoon while you're out shopping, you never know!" I said sarcastically.

"But the bastard Israelis never bothered to give us gas masks, so what difference does it make whether you're in or out of the house?" she got back at me half-seriously.

"No, Um Salim, just kidding."

"*Yalla,* come along," she repeated.

"No, never mind, Mother, I am fine. Just go with Salim and try to come back early—Salim and I have promised to visit Johni and Lamia."

"*Yalla, Mama* (Hurry up, Mama)!" yelled Salim from the car; he had lost patience waiting for her.

"I still think you should come," she mumbled as she closed the door behind her.

"And I think *you* should go," I mumbled back, with a big sigh.

I was totally depressed.

Perhaps I should have gone out, I thought to myself, but I didn't have the energy.

I went to the kitchen veranda and began trying to clear some space, in anticipation of the new food stocks that would arrive soon. I became even more depressed at that thought alone.

Every time the curfew was lifted, frantic crowds rushed to clear out every supermarket, store and bakery in Ramallah and al-Bireh.

The fear of hunger and the fear of endless curfew were soon replaced by the scraping clean of every shelf. All the food stores were complete madhouses; you needed to be a basketball player to successfully shop. The previous week in the Zabaneh store, various items had flown right over our heads. Some reached their targets, others were intercepted by unfriendly souls.

"Catch this one, Ayman," said a woman flinging food

items at her son, who had strategically located himself next to the cashier.

People were screaming at one another, passing food over the head of the overwhelmed cashier and piling it in front of him.

"Whose Pampers are these?" yelled Mitri, the shopkeeper.

"Mine, mine, I am coming. . . . No, Mama!* No more *chokalata* now," shouted a young mother from behind a shelf, dragging along her little girl, whose smiling face was totally smeared with Kit Kat.

"No, this is mine! I just put it here and you simply grabbed it."

"But this is my *Tnova* yogurt; yours was *Junedi*."

"Can't be! I never ever buy *Junedi* yogurt or any other Palestinian local product!" The two women, not missing a chance to establish political incorrectness, were screaming at one another now as items continued to fly through the air.

"*KHALAS* (FOR GOD'S SAKE, ENOUGH)!" came the exasperated voice of Maher, Mitri's brother. As one girl was helping her grandma get up from the floor, Maher was trying to sweep the oily, salty water running in the wake of an elderly man who had knocked over a huge wooden barrel of olives. The big splash had not deterred the old man from filling his two shaking palms with big black olives. Maher was carefully following the undulating line of oil and salt water dripping from the old man's palms.

*In Arabic, *mama* can refer to both mother and child.

"Can't you see the old woman just slipped because you flooded the store with slippery oil?"

"Whose fault is it if you have no bags to put the black olives in?"

Maher handed him a nylon bag.

Oh, God, I feel exhausted just at the thought of it all.

I was certain that everybody's house in Ramallah was starting to look like ours: a self-sufficient, shelfless mini-market. The food in the kitchen was spreading through the rest of the house. During curfew days, houses gradually metamorphosed into nothing but kitchens and bedrooms. Excessive eating, screaming at one another, and producing babies were the only three possible activities. No wonder the Israelis are totally obsessed with demographics.

Every time one of our neighbors baked *taboun* bread, she would make sure to send us a few loaves with one of her youngsters. I was sorting out the different types of bread in our own mini-market when I heard the footsteps of my mother-in-law.

"Ah . . . so you're back!"

"Oof . . . it was madness. I think you were right to stay behind. It is like *youm lieamah* (Judgment Day). Everybody in the supermarket is absolutely *majaneen* (crazy), as if there will never ever be food on this earth again: I don't understand," she complained as she handed me two huge bags.

"Go help Salim bring the rest of the food in. There is plenty more out in the car. We bought a few extra items just in case they don't lift the curfew for a few more days—you never know what might happen," she said in a worn-out voice.

"You certainly don't," I cried as I ran out to help Salim carry yet more bags into the kitchen.

"Come on, Suad, let's go visit Johni and Lamia. I need a break away from my mother. We can do all this when we come back."

"Bye, Mama."

"Empty the trunk, it is stacked with food."

"Never mind, we'll do it when we come back. We don't have much time: in forty minutes the curfew will be imposed again," I said as we both ran out.

"Don't be late, I don't like to be left alone," came the "motherly" command.

"Yes, Mother, we know."

"Why are you so late? There's hardly any time to visit Johni and Lamia. They have been calling to ask about you," complained Vera, Salim's cousin, violently lurching to one side as Salim drove off a bit recklessly after picking her up.

We sped frantically along al-Tireh Road. Salim suddenly hit the brake, and the car swerved, just avoiding a crash with another car coming in the opposite direction. There was no time for the two drivers to shout at one another; both kept driving.

Before we could even ring the bell, Lamia was at the door: "*Weenkun* (Where have you been)? We've been waiting for you. If we'd known you were going to be *this* late, we could have managed some more shopping. We could also have gone to see Johni's sick mother. Suzanne could not do any shopping at all, as she had to run and fetch Doctor Khalid. He has not been able to visit Johni's mother during curfew days. . . ."

What a relaxing visit this is turning out to be, I thought to myself.

"Come on in, sit down." We heard Johni's usual hospitable voice behind Lamia's back.

The three of us walked in and collapsed onto the comfortable sofas.

"Did you go shopping?"

"Yes, of course, it's still in the trunk—we didn't have time to unpack it. What about you?"

"Yes, some, but we had to hurry back to be here for you," she said, rather accusingly.

"Sorry I could not get you the cheesecake you like. Europa Pâtisserie has stopped delivering from Bethlehem," said Johni, concerned that his hospitality would not be seen as obsessive as usual.

"You know—because of the war," he added as he rushed off to the kitchen to fetch the carefully thought-out afternoon tea menu.

"Lamia, see what they would like to drink."

"It is OK, Johni, don't bother. We just came to see you and Lamia, and we don't need anything. We must get going in a short while anyway—we'll need to be on our way in fifteen minutes."

"At the most," said our already apprehensive hostess.

"No, no, you must try the cake I baked specially for you,

Vera. I also managed to get Earl Grey tea for Suad; I know she likes it. It was at least a ten-minute wait before I could reach it on the shelf at Zabaneh's. It was hell shopping there. You know how obsessive Siham Odeh can be. She was there and she wanted her balsamic vinegar. When she could not find it on the shelf, she insisted Mitri go and get it from the storeroom next door. Poor Mitri had to do it in spite of the demanding shoppers all around him. If I'd known you were going to be late, I could have gotten the green tea as well, but I really did not want to be late for you." Johni was giving all sorts of excuses in anticipation of any imperfections we noticed in his six-star service.

"Lamia, did you serve the drinks?" Johni asked worriedly from the kitchen. We heard the clacking of the teacups. "Johni, stop fussing; there is hardly time for tea, just bring it out here quickly."

We were all now totally engrossed in our host's preparations.

"Do you think Saddam will use any chemical or nuclear warheads?" Salim asked, trying to lighten the intense atmosphere.

"Johni, we really have to leave; it is getting dark and we must get going before they impose the curfew again," said Vera very anxiously.

"No, wait, it's all here; ready," came Johni's unconvincing voice, mixed with the tinkles of plates, forks and cups.

Soon the disjointed conversation and its long pauses were interrupted by the screeching of the tea trolley, which had diagonal wheels and had certainly seen better days.

"Once things settle down a bit we must buy a new trolley," said Johni in his ever-apologetic tone. From the tilted trolley, Johni started taking one item at a time and placing it on the coffee table right in front of us: the Armenian ceramic nut bowls, the earth-colored teapot with matching cups and saucers, the sugar bowl and milk jug, the carrot cake on a silver plate, the small pottery plates with red and green napkins in between, probably left over from Christmas. Once the middle coffee table was filled, he started placing things on the three smaller side tables.

"Wow, Johni! It's as if there isn't a war!" said Vera appreciatively.

"Our life is a series of wars," replied Johni.

We quickly swallowed the cake, gulped the hot tea and with burning tongues and full mouths, bid them farewell.

"Please, Vera, take the carrot cake with you. Lamia and I are on a diet. . . . Please take it away—otherwise we'll eat it in one go. We've both gained so much weight during this curfew."

Bye . . .

Bye . . .

Bye . . .

Bye . . .

Bye . . .

The three of us were tremendously anxious when we realized it was ten minutes past curfew. I jumped into the backseat, Vera and Salim into the front seats, and we drove away at top speed.

It was a very dark night; the rain and thick mist made the

driving nerve-racking. We were the only souls on the streets of Ramallah, which added to the spookiness of the situation.

It was when we'd almost hit it that we realized the object in front of us was an Israeli Army jeep.

My heart sank.

Salim turned pale.

Vera froze with fear.

All we could see were the barrels of the two rifles pointed at us. It did not take long to work out we were in deep trouble.

"Stop the engine and get out of the car immediately," shouted one of the soldiers.

Salim and Vera were out of the car in no time. I was stuck in the back, as I could not reach the lever to flip forward the front seat. I have always hated two-door cars.

"You in the backseat, get out."

"I can't reach to open the door," I replied, while trying hard to reach the front-seat lever.

"Never mind, stay where you are," said one of the soldiers as his friend body-searched Salim. Vera stood still in the pouring rain. Soon afterwards, she was asked to hand in her ID and go back to the car.

"Open the trunk," screamed one of the soldiers at Salim.

Oh, God! The shopping bags, I thought to myself.

As Salim opened the trunk, the two soldiers jumped back.

"What is this?" asked one of them as he pointed his rifle at the multitude of shopping bags.

"My mother's shopping," answered Salim with a nervous smile and an ever-guilty face.

"Get them out," demanded one of the soldiers as he nervously moved the tip of his rifle between Salim's head and my mother-in-law's shopping.

"Can I get out and help?" I asked, trying to defuse the mounting tension.

"*Hajjeh* (old woman), just stay where you are," answered the soldier, in the condescending tone often used by Israeli soldiers when addressing Palestinians, especially women.

He looked at me through the wide-open window at the back. He was right there, his head just next to mine.

My hand could easily have reached his throat.

Hajjeh! *Motherfucker, it's true I could be your mother's age or even older, but I am definitely not a* hajjeh ya hayawan—*not an old woman, stupid.*

I was so offended that I totally forgot all about Salim's impossible mission to empty all the shopping bags in the pouring rain.

One thing Israeli soldiers must be taught, among many other things, is to never ever use the word *hajjeh*. It makes the Occupation doubly painful.

I don't know what happened to me at that moment. The word *hajjeh*, the immaturity in the shrieking voice of the boyish soldier, the haziness and darkness, all stirred in me the frustrations of weeks of curfews, the aggravation of months' preparation for the Gulf War, the anger and resentment caused by the twenty-four-year-long occupation, the decades of unfulfilled aspirations, the eternal yearning for normality.

I was contemplating confrontation strategies.

Angry words or, God forbid, violent acts from an early-menopausal woman under occupation may lead to unbearable consequences, if not for herself, then at least for her waterlogged husband.

I stuck my head out of the back window and stared at the brainless soldier. Salim was still moving back and forth, clearing the trunk of shopping bags. As soon as he had finished, the soldier shouted, "*Roough* (Go) stand against that wall," in broken Arabic.

With the tip of his rifle the soldier was still fiddling around in the empty trunk. I twisted my head half a circle towards him and with owllike eyes I started staring at him.

I could not help it. I was so full of anger I decided just to go for it. My head was literally an inch or two away from his.

"Why are you staring at me?" the soldier objected.

I kept looking him in the eye with an expressionless face.

"Stop looking at me!" screamed the easily rattled soldier.

Fucker, I thought to myself. So irritated by a stare!

I wonder what your reaction would have been if you had lived under occupation for as many years as I had, or if your shopping rights, like all your other rights, were violated day and night, or if the olive trees in your grandfather's orchards had been uprooted, or if your village had been bulldozed, or if your house had been demolished, or if your sister could not reach her school, or if your brother had been given three life sentences, or if your mother had given birth at a checkpoint, or if you had stood in line for days in the hot August summers waiting for your work permit, or if you could not reach your beloved ones in Arab East Jerusalem. . . .

A stare, and you lose your mind!

"Did you hear what I said? Stop staring at me! Are you deaf?" repeated the violated soldier.

I am neither deaf nor blind nor mute, young man. Like the rest of us, I have learned how to act deaf, seem blind, pretend to be mute every time I encounter one of you in our towns, our streets, our houses, our living rooms or even our bedrooms.

Do you want to know how I felt when I acted deaf, the day your fellow soldiers insulted the old man at the checkpoint?

Do you want to know how I felt when I seemed blind as your colleagues were beating up my students, when I was on my way to teach at Birzeit University?

Or would you rather know what was going on in my mind as one of your beloved soldiers screamed in distorted Arabic at the women standing next to me in the pouring rain, while we begged for our residency permits so that we could live with our husbands and families?

Do you NOW understand why we act deaf, blind and mute for most of our lives?

Do you realize what it would be like if we started acting like normal human beings every day, every hour, every minute or second in which you have violated our rights?

Do you realize what kind of will (and humiliation) it takes to teach ourselves not to hear, not to see and not to speak up?

That is exactly why the whole world is taken by surprise whenever we decide to see, hear and speak up, every one or two decades.

It happened in 1929.

And in 1936.

And last in 1987.

The last time we heard, saw and spoke up, you were only fourteen.

"I said stop staring at me!" shrieked the soldier.

By that time both Salim and Vera were aware of my game.

"What's going on?" came Salim's edgy voice from a distance.

I could not have cared less. I just kept staring at the soldier, who had now stopped fiddling with the spare tire in the trunk.

"Stop it, Suad, I don't think it's the right time for that," pleaded a desperate Salim.

My body was twisted, my neck stretched like a giraffe's and my already big eyes wide open with an even bigger stare. I was not in the mood to listen to either of them, nor to Vera's scared begging from the front seat.

"Suad, please stop it," Salim pleaded. "You always get us in trouble with Israeli soldiers. This is not the time for it; we have to go back home before it's too dark. You know my mother is all by herself at home. . . . We are not in a position to take risks."

I was entranced. My eyes were fixed on the Israeli soldier's eyes.

"This is the last time I'm going to tell you to stop looking at me, do you understand?" came the final command of the soldier.

"*Uba'dein* (Just stop it)," said Salim, his voice rising.

"How is she related to you?" asked the soldier.

"She is my wife," answered Salim, none too proudly.

"Then ask your wife to stop staring at me."

"Suad, stop staring at him."

In vain.

"Suad. *Khalas*," said Vera in a high-pitched voice.

"So this WIFE of yours does not listen to you, does she?" Now came the macho man-to-man talk.

I did not turn to look at Salim's reaction, as I was still mesmerized by staring at the soldier, straight in the eye.

"OK, get back in your car and wait; *mush 'aref trabi maratak* (you don't even have the power to force your wife to behave)," remarked the soldier, in an attempt to belittle Salim.

"You see what I mean" was the first thing Salim said as he opened the car door and got in.

"Is that what you wanted, Suad?" blamed Vera, Salim's cousin.

Poor Salim, I thought to myself. Rainwater was dripping all over the car seat; Salim, unlike the soldiers, did not have a raincoat. He was soaking and looked really miserable. I felt bad, but I did not regret my passive resistance to occupation.

I must admit it was not really being called *hajjeh*.

This was the least I could do to get back at them.

I was taking a long-overdue revenge.

A few minutes passed before the soldier disappeared into one of the two jeeps parked in the mist of al-Tireh Road.

We were left alone in the car. Salim and Vera started moaning as loudly as the wind outside.

And I burst into hysterical laughter.

"I don't think this is funny," said Salim.

They both sat there in deadly silence, while I rolled round in the backseat, laughing.

"You always do silly things and I end up paying the price. Remember when the soldiers tried to confiscate our car?" Salim reprimanded me.

I was still giggling in the back when the soldier appeared again out of the mist. He leaned towards Salim's window and ordered, "Follow me."

"What about the shopping bags? Why don't you say farewell to your mother's groceries, Salim?" I screamed with laughter from the back as I waved good-bye.

I could see Salim and Vera looking at each other.

We were soon under escort by the two military jeeps, one in front and one behind.

Being led by a military jeep certainly made driving through the thick fog much easier.

As we entered the premises of the Ramallah military compound, the "Civil Administration" headquarters, the two jeeps stopped and our beloved soldier appeared again.

"Get out," he instructed Salim.

Vera and I watched as a soaked Salim disappeared in the dark mazes of the military compound.

It did not take long before I broke the silence.

"Can you imagine what the soldier is going to tell his commander?" I laughed in an attempt to cheer Vera up.

" 'His wife *could not* stop looking at me,' " I said, trying to imitate the soldier's macho teenage voice.

Once again I burst into hysterics.

Realizing the absurdity of the situation, Vera finally joined me in frantic laughter.

We were soon concocting various Kafkaesque scenes for Salim's "Trial."

We were on the fifth scene when Salim appeared.

In no time, the two hysterics had become three.

Our dry senses of humor were soon wet, as tears of laughter poured down our cheeks.

"Tell us what happened!" both Vera and I excitedly implored.

"You would not believe it. The soldier took me in . . . ha . . . ha . . . ha . . ." Salim cracked up, unable to finish his sentence.

"Come on, Salim, tell us."

"OK."

He gave it another try.

"The soldiers took me inside and made me wait. As other soldiers passed by, they would look at me suspiciously, trying to figure out what had brought me here at this hour (when the whole town was under curfew) and in the middle of a nasty war. Much later, the Israeli soldier came back and asked me to accompany him. We both stood in front of Captain Roni's office." Salim cracked up once more.

"Salim, stop it! Tell us what happened."

"The soldier knocked at the door of Captain Roni's office and waited, then he knocked again, and we heard Captain Roni's reply from inside.

"'Who is it? Come on in.' The soldier opened the door and hesitantly stepped in. I dragged my feet behind him. Captain Roni was on the phone, we both stood still and tall in front of his desk, like two good soldiers on duty, waiting for him to finish his long phone conversation.

"You know my Hebrew is not so fantastic," added Salim. Salim started imitating the head commander in broken Arabic.

"'Aghea Waw (Area O), yes, yes, Scud missiles . . . little Baghdad . . . Palestinians banging on electric poles, screaming from rooftops, perhaps another week or two of war . . . Saddam . . . Patriots, not really working.'

"Suddenly, Captain Roni, who had been staring at the two of us all along, moved the phone receiver away from his mouth, looked at the soldier and asked, 'What is it, Rafi?'

"Rafi, the soldier, looked at his commander and said hesitantly, 'His wife was looking at me.'

"'WHAT?' answered Captain Roni, totally astounded.

"'His wife was staring at me,' he repeated.

"'Whose wife?'

"'His.' He pointed towards me.

"'Who is he?'

"Not knowing who I was, the soldier pulled out my ID and read out loud, 'Salim Edmon Elias Tamari.' He looked at his commander, hoping to somehow gain his sympathy.

"'And what about Shalom Edi Elion Tamari?' asked Captain Roni impatiently, still holding the phone receiver.

"'His wife would not stop looking at me.'

"'At *you*!'

"'Yes, sir, at me.'

"'Why?'

"'Ask him—I don't know.'

"'And why was your wife looking at Rafi?' inquired Captain Roni, unconvinced.

"As I took my time searching for the impossible answer, I was saved by a shriek from Captain Roni, which cut through the thunder and lightning and filled the skies of Ramallah.

"'You two, get the hell out of here. Don't you realize we are at war? The Jewish people are threatened by Saddam's chemical weapons and Scud missiles. . . . You stupid boys, get out of my sight . . . NOW! . . .'"

"We both turned our backs swiftly and before we knew it we were outside Captain Roni's office in the long, dark corridor. His screams could still be heard. We stared at one another, then he handed me my ID, and I walked away."

As we drove home in the dark and under curfew, we replayed the different scenarios of Salim's "Trial." We began by imagining next morning's headlines.

The Israeli Army press spokesman was diverted from war news to announce:

"Professor Tamari, from Birzeit University, the nesting place of *teghogh* (terror), was sentenced to six months' imprisonment, as he had failed to deter his wife from firing stares at an Israeli soldier on duty in Judaea and Samaria.

"From past experience, we can tell that this particular type of stare often takes place just minutes before life-threatening situations arise. Six months' imprisonment is meant as a preemptive measure," added the Israeli Army spokesman, who for security reasons insisted his name be withheld.

No one ever asked why it was the husband, and not the criminal wife, who was to be punished.

7

The Promised Gas Masks

February 1991

The doorbell rang unexpectedly under curfew. My eyes half open, I dragged myself up on my stiff bare feet, and went to answer it.

"What is it, Hasan?" I asked the eleven-year-old son of the neighbors.

"*Khalto*, hurry up, you and *Ammo* (Uncle) Salim. You must go fetch your gas masks."

"What gas masks?" I inquired, still half-asleep.

"The Israeli Army has decided to distribute gas masks for our neighborhood . . . *only* our neighborhood," he added.

"Why? Has Saddam decided to hit our neighborhood? We are not little Baghdad, are we?" I was trying hard to make sense of what Hasan had said.

"I don't know, *Khalto,* my mother asked me to tell you to go fetch your gas masks. . . . She saw all the neighbors go out to fetch their gas masks except you and *Ammo*," he added.

"But the war has almost ended."

"I don't know, *Khalto,*" replied Hasan, sneaking away in an attempt to evade my nasty early-morning mood.

"Have they lifted the curfew?" I asked.

"No," came Hasan's reply from a distance.

"Then . . . how are we to fetch the gas masks?"

"I don't know, *Khalto,* talk to my mother if you have more questions." I heard the echo of Hasan's voice.

I went back to bed, and tried to get some more sleep and forget all about the gas masks.

Soon after, the phone rang:

"Hi, this is Haifa."

"Yes, yes, Hasan came by and told me, but I did not quite believe him. They did not lift the curfew?"

"A military jeep came by and said we must get our gas masks."

"At six in the morning? It is almost noon now," I said, looking at my watch. "OK, Haifa. I'll wake Salim up and we'll come by."

"What's going on?" asked Salim as he stretched out diagonally in bed.

"We must go and get our gas masks."

"Who needs gas masks?"

The four of us, Haifa, Gabi, Salim and I, were marching along the middle of the al-Irsal road towards the military compound in Ramallah.

"You know, most of our neighbors went early to fetch

their gas masks, almost six hours have passed now, and none has made it back," said Gabi in his tranquil voice when we were halfway to our target.

I didn't quite know what to make of this piece of news. I was already anxious about going out while the curfew was still imposed, thinking about the people who had been killed or injured in the past, as a result of breaking curfews.

If forced to venture out during a curfew, one has to be extremely cautious and low-key.

Walking with Gabi and Haifa was certainly a risk. Gabi is almost six feet five inches tall, and has a large head with exaggerated features. His sienna red jacket did not help. Haifa is my height, five feet six inches, but her huge bosoms and wide shoulders give her a commanding appearance. Her soprano voice rose and fell, contrasting sharply with Gabi's bass and with the deadly silence of Ramallah under curfew. Gabi and Haifa are in the Jerusalem Choir. Unlike the three of us, Salim's size was not a liability, but his perpetually guilty facial expressions would not be an asset if we were arrested. His silence contributed to the mounting tension.

Wouldn't it be tragic to be shot while trying to save ourselves by getting gas masks? I thought to myself.

"I don't understand why they don't lift the curfew or simply distribute the gas masks," I said to Gabi, who, unlike me, seemed to be totally relaxed—moving his long arms and legs at full stride.

"Come on, Suad, you mean everything else makes sense to you?"

"No, but this is absolutely ridiculous."

"Living under a curfew for thirty-six days is not ridiculous, not giving Palestinians in the West Bank and Gaza gas masks is not ridiculous, giving the Arabs in Israel out-of-date gas masks is not ridiculous, the absolute madness and hysteria about Saddam's chemical and nuclear warheads are not ridiculous, bringing your mother-in-law and my ninety-year-old mother to live with us in sealed rooms day and night is not ridiculous . . . NOT RIDICULOUS?" Gabi seemed to have lost it.

"OK, OK, Gabi, let's not get carried away," I said, although I agreed with him. I think it was the combination of his wife and mother that he could not take. I was in total sympathy.

It was not long after this that the utter silence was broken by the screams of the crowd and the sounds of army loudspeakers coming from a distance.

"I think we can do without the gas masks," said Salim.

With increasing anxiety, we continued walking towards the army loudspeakers, in the direction of the military compound.

"*Ta'al* (Come this way)!" shouted an Israeli soldier through his loudspeaker, the moment he saw us from a distance.

"I think we could have done without the gas masks," Salim noted again.

As we were obeying orders, marching towards the Israeli soldier, we could see a portion of a bus engulfed by the crowd that was pressing in on it; some were crammed inside, others were hanging from the windows and doors, a few more youngsters were dangling from the two bars at the back.

"No one will get a gas mask unless you all stand in order," the soldier shouted again through his loudspeaker, though he stood just six and a half feet away from the desperate crowd.

What order? I thought to myself.

"I think we should go back home," Salim said.

As we got closer, some of the crowd started looking familiar; there was Abu el-'Abed, the kerosene man, without his horse and carriage; there was Abu Mazen, the policeman, without his uniform; there was Munir, the staff nurse, without his white gown; there was Kamal, the shopkeeper, who had gained some weight since I last saw him a few weeks previously. It took some effort to place people even though they were all *wlad haritna* (our neighbors).

"Why is he using the loudspeaker? He is only six and a half feet away. Does he think we're deaf?" I said at the top of my voice, trying to outspeak the crowd and the loudspeaker.

"Even if we're not *turshan* (deaf), we soon will be," came the answer from a young man whose body was dangling from the window of the bus.

Some people were trying to get on the bus; others, who were suffocating, were trying to get off the bus.

The four of us stood there trying to figure out what it was all about; Gabi was bending over talking to a truly deaf neighbor, Abu Maher, who was used to making lots of hand gestures. He covered his face with his two trembling palms, which I understood to mean gas masks, then he pointed to the bus, which I understood to mean: those who want to get

gas masks have to get on the bus; then he pointed to the soldier with the loudspeaker as he moved his two hands together and away from his ears, then Abu Maher pointed again
towards the bus but now with a down sign. The soldier
wanted people to get off the bus.

I came close to Gabi and Abu Maher and yelled, "Why is
the bus here anyway? The Civil Administration compound is
just across the road."

Abu Maher raised his thick eyebrows, flipped his voluptuous lower lip and twisted open both trembling palms.

I felt a hand on my shoulder and I looked around. It was
Emile, a friend whose house was just there. Actually, half of
the commotion was taking place in his front garden. I felt
enormous relief the moment I saw him.

"Hiiiiiiiiiiii, Emile, *keeeeeefak* (how are you)?" I gave Emile
a big kiss and an even bigger hug.

"As you see," he shouted at the top of his voice. "If you
can't beat them, join them." He had a big beaming smile on
his long bearded face.

All of a sudden I noticed that Emile was holding a ther-
mos of coffee and small paper cups.

"What is this?" I inquired.

"Well, I decided to take part in this 'tragicomedy,' since
the stage is in our front garden."

All of a sudden I remembered Emile's talents. He is not
only a good photographer, but a gifted actor as well. Though
handsome, his misfortune is that he looks exactly like the
Israeli West Bank general commander Amram Mitzna. We
were always concerned that he might be stabbed one day by

mistake. But Emile also enjoys the Israeli Army salutes he often gets from Israeli soldiers.

And here was Mitzna making life under occupation and curfew more tolerable by offering us Turkish coffee.

I decided to be Mitzna's assistant.

"Here, have some coffee," I said as I passed on the paper cups to members of our neighborhood crowd. Emile continued to pour the coffee from high in the air, imitating the traditional coffeeshops in the old city of Jerusalem where he grew up.

"*Yakhkh* . . . why no sugar?" complained Abu Nader as he spat the remains on the ground.

"*'Ammi,* this is not a *'urus* (Uncle, this is not a wedding),"* came Emile's irritated voice.

"*'Urus ou nuss* (Of course it's a wedding). They will soon be giving us gas masks," insisted Abu Nader.

"*'Aza, 'aza, fahim 'aza* (It's a funeral, a funeral, you understand, a funeral), that's why there's no sugar. Give me back the coffee," yelled Emile, pretending to snatch the coffee cup away from Abu Nader.

Emile burst out laughing and patted Abu Nader on the shoulder. With Emile, you never know when acting ends and real life begins.

Mitzna and I continued our little act, mingling among the crowd.

"*Ahwet, 'aza tafadal* (Funeral coffee, have some)," and we

---

* In Arabic, *wedding* can also refer to happy occasions. Sweet coffee is served at weddings and bitter coffee at funerals.

would both giggle as I stretched my hand out with a cup of coffee.

"*Falcom, 'ala halkum* (Bad omen, stop it)," was the frequent reply.

"Perhaps I should go and add the twenty-kilo sack of sugar I bought yesterday—is it not enough that I've wasted all the coffee on you? The worst part is that you think this is a wedding; *you* Palestinians are never defeated, that's how YOU lost Palestine," continued Emile.

"What do you mean, '*you* Palestinians'? Aren't *you* one of us?" screamed robust Ibrahim, our neighbor, who had just been released from prison. For a moment, I suspected he was about to commit a terrible act against Emile "Mitzna." It was difficult for me to figure out how serious or playful the situation was. Ibrahim's subtle smile put my heart to rest.

"Get in line. All of you get off the bus and stand in line here, otherwise you will never get your gas masks." The Israeli soldier was still at it.

"No coffee for you, bastard," I said in a low voice.

I don't know what it is with Israeli soldiers. They all have a fetish for making Palestinians stand in an orderly line. They complicate our lives with all sorts of permits, make them unbearably chaotic, then insist we stand in straight lines.

"No one will get their *tasreekh* (permit) unless you stand in a straight line."

"No one will get their *hawiyyeh* back unless you stand in a straight line."

"No one will pass through the checkpoint unless you stand in a straight line."

"No one will cross the Allenby Bridge unless you stand in a straight line."

"No one . . . unless . . . a straight line."

Have you ever seen a natural straight line?

"*Ya 'ammi* (For God's sake), we are *fawwdah, ah fawwdah* (chaotic, simply chaotic). Why can't we ever stand in a straight line?" came the comment of a middle-aged man.

"*Ya 'ammi,* just stand in line and we will soon get our gas masks. We have been in this mess for hours now," came the voice of another wise man.

"I think we're better off without the gas masks," insisted Salim.

All of a sudden Sami and 'Ali, the two youngsters from the neighborhood committee, appeared and took command. They got everyone off the bus, including those hanging off the back and the sides, and in no time the shouting crowd was transformed into a still-shouting but straight line, so straight that some were miles away, almost back home.

"OK," said the Israeli soldier, now that we were all in order, "now get on the bus, *wakhad, wakhad mafkhoum* (one by one, you understand)." He sounded more like a headmaster than a soldier.

"*Mafkhoum* (We understand)," some of us repeated, imitating his distorted Arabic.

About one-fifth of us made it onto the bus, while the rest were trying hard to maintain the straight line.

"OK, turn round and drive into the compound," the soldier instructed the bus driver.

"But we're right there," said the driver, pointing towards the military compound just across the road.

"I said turn round!" screamed the soldier.

"OK!" obeyed the driver.

As the bus started moving we heard one fellow say from behind: "You think they're going to give us gas masks, ha? This is the *Transfer* Bus to Jordan." We all burst into hysterical laughter.

"Yes, that's how in 1948 we were transferred out of Nazareth." Another even more hysterical laugh.

"You thought you were lucky making it to the bus, ha?" A third burst of hysteria.

"We Palestinians are so stupid. They always manage to fool us. We never learn from past experiences," joined in one woman.

"Right, why put us on a bus if they only wanted to give us gas masks? They could have simply distributed them. We have been here for eight hours now."

"Say good-bye to your relatives—you may never see them again." As he waved his hand out of the window, we all followed suit.

"We are gone until UN Resolution 194 concerning the right of refugees to return home is implemented," joked another.

"So glad my mother-in-law is not with us," said Haifa.

"So glad Um Salim will not be transferred with us," I added.

"You see, transfer is not such a bad idea after all," said Gabi.

The bus moved a few feet, just enough to make a U-turn, and stopped on the opposite side of Emile's house, right in front of the closed gates of the military compound. At that point the straight geometrical line gained life again by returning to what it once was: an amorphous screaming crowd.

As we waited, some inside the bus, some outside, two more Israeli soldiers appeared from the compound.

"Ah . . . *wa akheeran* (at last)." A big sigh from Gabi.

"I am dying to hold a gas mask. I've only seen them on TV," said a young boy accompanying his mother.

"*Yamma* Saber (Saber, my son), they make you look like creatures from Mars, I don't know how you breathe with them. I am not wearing one. I would rather die from the gas than look so ridiculous," answered his mother.

"Can I have two, then?" said Saber with great excitement.

We were all glancing sideways, watching the movements of the two Israeli soldiers. As they moved in and out of the gate of the compound, our hopes rose and fell again. Finally, they both approached our bus, bringing—we hoped—good news. One of them came closer, looked at the bus driver and started waving his arms.

"What does this one want now?" inquired the bus driver.

"Go back," said Abu Maher, who had strategically located himself on the seat immediately behind the driver.

"Back where?" asked the driver.

"Back," repeated Abu Maher.

One soldier kept moving his arms, while the other soldier picked up the loudspeaker and started imposing a curfew that had never been lifted in the first place:

"*Mamnu' il tajawol hatta ish'arin akhar* (Movement is forbidden until further notice)."

"See, we could have done without the stupid gas masks," said Salim as we became part of the crowd hurriedly going back home empty-handed.

Several days later, the Gulf War ended. None of the Palestinians living in the West Bank or Gaza Strip were given gas masks.

All the Israelis were given gas masks.

Four Israelis died as a result of injecting themselves with atropine out of fear of Saddam's chemical weapons.

In the field behind our house I recognized little Saber, playing soldiers with his friends while holding a gas mask. I wanted to ask him where he got it from but I didn't.

8

Palestina Vulgaris

A few minutes after Salim left in his car, the phone rang. At the other end was Rami's familiar unsettling voice: "Hello, Suad." I took note of the fact that I was no longer his auntie.

"Hello, Rami, it's been a while," I said.

"Yes, I have been busy with my job in Tel Aviv."

I stopped short of shouting, *What* job? It must have been my silence that made Rami quickly explain, "I have been working in a jaiz (the Hebrew pronunciation for *jazz*) club in Tel Aviv."

"Oh, jazz, how nice!" I said with a big sense of relief. That's a better way of collaborating with the Israelis, I thought to myself.

"Suad, I have something for you. Can I come and see you?"

"Sorry, Rami, I'm on my way out." My jumpiness at being trapped in the fifty-seventh episode of Rami's (and his mother, Um Zahi's) soap opera made me lie instinctively.

"I'll just deliver it and go away," insisted Rami.

"OK," I said in a resigned tone.

"I'll be there right away," said Rami eagerly.

I hung up the receiver and dashed to my bedroom, and in less than a minute my white nightgown and embroidered slippers were exchanged for any garment my slightly trembling hands could snatch.

I managed to go out and throw myself on the sofa in the front veranda. I had plenty of time to allow my pulse to return to normal, but also to realize how ridiculous I looked. The nonmatching colors of my red-and-yellow floral skirt and Salim's blue-and-grey-striped shirt might easily reveal my deception.

I positioned myself on the sofa so that I could see Rami the minute he stepped out of his house. There he was, carrying the not-so-small *something* in his strong arms. The upper half of Rami's body and the lower part of his face had disappeared behind the something, which was wrapped in glittering white and silver paper. The reflections of the sun on the gift wrap added to my edginess. I started guessing what the something could be. Could it be a saxophone that Rami stole from his jazz club in Tel Aviv? Stealing "things" (especially cars) from Israelis was one way some Palestinian workers got back at the Israelis for stealing our land and homes (we've got to do much more stealing before we get even).

I pretended not to see Rami as he twisted his body to get through our garden gate. I could have helped him by saving him the trouble of ringing the doorbell, but did not.

"Come on in," I said, as I walked slowly towards the door.

"Rami, what *is* this? Didn't we agree no more presents?"

"It's just a simple gift," he replied as he placed it on the table just inside the front door. He looked at me and smiled.

Not respectful of Arab gift etiquette (whereby you pretend not to see the gift, and thus totally ignore it), I immediately opened it. I could not believe my eyes.

It was a huge tableau of Mecca.

As I was admiring the tableau, which measured almost 20 by 30 inches, Rami drew my attention to its additional virtues.

"You can plug it into the electricity," he instructed me as he inserted the plug in the nearest socket. There was Mecca's Black Stone in the middle of tiny, twinkling-on-and-off red and green bulbs.

It was so kitsch, I fell in love with it.

The excitement over the tableau did not make me forget my lie. I had an appointment. I had to go.

I did not know what kind of face Salim would make, this time, when he saw Rami's latest gift. I still laugh every time I recall Salim's funny faces, the way he rolled his droopy eyes upwards, whenever Rami brought me gifts, especially red roses.

Later, as Salim and I were enjoying ourselves admiring the twinkling Mecca, all of a sudden I had a chilling thought:

"You know what, Salim? This Mecca is bugged, I swear to God it must be bugged," I said with utter conviction.

"What?" Salim inquired in his cool, cynical way.

"I bet you anything this Mecca is bugged," I repeated.

"Stop being silly," Salim said, slowly realizing how serious my suspicions were.

There was absolutely no way to convince me otherwise. My sixth sense told me it was bugged and I fully trusted my sixth sense. There was no way for me to find out whether I was right because I and the others around me are technologically retarded, especially when it comes to the espionage techniques used by the Israeli Mossad.

"I think you're being completely silly. But if you're so paranoid, just get rid of it."

"But how can I throw Mecca in the garbage?" I begged Salim for a solution.

Weary of my paranoia and Rami's continuous incursions into our lives, Salim walked away.

The Mecca glittered red and green.

I could not sleep that night. Why would Rami give me a tableau of Mecca, when he knew that I was a leftist and religion was not my strong point? What are Rami and his big bosses trying to tell me? Or is he trying to tell Salim something? The long hours of the winter night only prolonged my hallucinations.

The tableau was put away in the attic.

Il Giorno delle Donne 1992

It was a rainy day at the end of winter. Neither the rain, nor the Israeli soldiers standing at a distance, nor the soaked banner with dripping red ink, under which the Communist activist Amal Khresheh stood with her hissing loudspeaker, prevented her or the other women activists from screaming their heads off:

La ya Rabin la, la lil ihtilal la (No to Rabin No,
     No to Occupation No).
No to Rabin No, No to Occupation No.
No to Rabin No, No to Occupation No.
No . . . No, No . . . No.

The repeated slogans of all the women demonstrators marching around Amal gave a few seconds' rest to the protruding veins of her thick neck. She swung her heavy, robust figure, and the blood rushing into her wide red cheeks accentuated her full-moon face.

The "No to Rabin," and the "No to Occupation" and every now and then the "Yes for Women" slogans (understood by most as anti-men slogans) were to mark International Women's Day. Neither the Palestinian women demonstrating in the middle of al-Manarah Square in Ramallah nor the Israeli male soldiers standing in full alert behind their pointed rifles in armored jeeps knew what my Italian book, *The Complete Idiot's Guide to Learning Italian* (given to me by Mahmoud, a friend of mine, when every other attempt to learn *la bella lingua* failed), had taught me:

> March 8 is celebrated internationally as *il giorno delle donne* (Women's Day) to commemorate the Triangle Shirtwaist Fire. On 25 March 1911, this tragic event in New York City took the lives of 146 factory workers, mostly young Italian and Jewish immigrant women. The tragedy led to the creation of

many labor laws governing the welfare and
safety of workers.

If any one of them, especially the Israeli male soldiers, realized that today's celebration was in memory of the young
Italian (who cares!) and Jewish immigrant women, perhaps
they would have behaved differently.

The anti-Occupation slogans and the chanting were certainly not about the tragic events in New York in 1911 which
took the lives of 146 Triangle Shirtwaist workers but about
the tragic events in the Occupied Territories which had already taken the lives of thousands of young Palestinian men,
women and children, most of them from refugee camps.

Unlike the tragic event of 1911, which led to the creation
of many laws governing the welfare and safety of workers,
none of the Palestinian tragic events have resulted in welfare
and safety laws.

Amal and the rest of the Palestinian women demonstrators had made up their minds long ago about what Women's
Day in Ramallah was all about:

It is the *one day* when women can prove to all men, Palestinians and Israelis alike, that they can single-handedly
organize (and take credit for) one of the biggest anti-
Occupation demonstrations.

It is the *one day* when screaming and shouting is a healthy
outlet for releasing the frustration, pain and agony
caused by endless decades of Israeli occupation.

It is the *one day* when women can express their anger about their lives. And what better target than male Israeli soldiers!

It is the *one day* when women compete with one another more than any other day.

It is the *one day* when it is difficult to define who the enemy is.

It is also the *one day* when Palestinian men see Israeli soldiers beat up and shoot at Palestinian women but won't do much about it.

It is the *one day* when women demonstrate their anti-men feelings in disguise, under the "End of Occupation" banner.

Perhaps that explains why often only four or at most five men (in addition to the Israeli soldiers) take part in Ramallah's Women's Day demonstration: Abu Nabil, the head of the Ramallah police; Jalil Hilal, an economist who's got no money; Sami Nofal, a writer and a witness to most, if not all, Palestinian political activities; and Salim Tamari, a sociologist who simply adores women. All were men in midlife and in complete denial, like the leftist parties they once belonged to.

But that day, Palestinian men also did not do much when Roger Heacock, a French professor of history at Birzeit University, was beaten up and arrested by the Israeli soldiers.

Professor Heacock was then accused of organizing the

Palestinian Women's Day demonstration. Many Palestinian men wanted to believe it was so. And most Israeli soldiers swore it under oath at Professor Heacock's trial.

None of us could even jokingly break the news about the accusations against Roger to Amal Khresheh. The Israeli soldiers, like the men of her own party, would never, ever give her credit, nor, for that matter, acknowledge her hard work. It seemed that her shrieking voice coming through the static of the old-fashioned loudspeaker was not enough evidence that she was one of the main women organizers, if not *the* organizer.

Life has once again been proven to be unfair. Men always end up taking credit for things they didn't do.

Roger, his wife, Laura, and their four mischievous children have lived in Ramallah for many years. Because they live close to al-Manarah Square, Roger and the other members of the Heacock family have witnessed almost all of the daily anti-Occupation confrontations with the Israeli soldiers. Only a few days earlier, Roger had helped a Palestinian boy, who had thrown a stone at the Israeli soldiers, hide away as the soldiers came running after him.

It happened that 8 March was the *one day* each year that Roger had full responsibility for his four kids, as Laura was busy organizing the Women's Day demonstration. Roger was on his way to buy apple juice for Jamal's upset stomach when an Israeli soldier jumped off his jeep, came up running, grabbed Roger and started beating him. Other soldiers joined in.

It turned out that the Israeli soldier had a good memory but a bad conscience. It was somehow easier for the Israeli soldiers to prove (and find witnesses for) their accusation that Roger had organized the Women's Day demonstration than that he had hidden the nine-year-old boy. What difference did it make what Roger had or had not done—as long as he was proven guilty?

Until his trial, Roger was thrown into a small, crowded cell under the staircase of the Ramallah police station. During his four-day stay, Roger made a few close friends, including a *sheikh* from the village of Hizma who was accused of killing three members of his own family. The *sheikh* kept promising to take Roger on picnics with the remaining members of his family, once they were out of prison.

Another of Roger's friends was a deaf-mute man from the nearby town of Betunia. He had been arrested together with his donkey for breaking into a supermarket and stealing a donkey's load of cigarette cartons. What bothered the deaf-mute most was that he *and his donkey* had been recognized, even though he had camouflaged his and the donkey's heads in black-and-white *kuffiyyehs* (traditional Palestinian headscarves). Both the man and his donkey were accused of illicit trafficking.

Roger's lawyer was told that he could be released on bail. But none of us seemed to have the two thousand dollars needed for Roger's temporary release. A party and an auction were organized. Even if the auction did not succeed in raising the funds for Roger's bail, it would certainly raise our morale.

While Sotheby's Auction House in London emphasizes the antique value of its items, we decided our auction would emphasize the kitsch value of our items.

Rami's bugged Mecca tableau was brought down from the attic after having been abandoned for quite some time. A year of attic silence followed by the sudden noises of Roger's auction party must have been mind-boggling for Mossad.

Have them figure *this* one out!

The multitudes of the Heacocks' friends and acquaintances met at Roger's house. That evening confirmed my long-held belief that Palestine is the world's center for kitsch.

The auction's theme was *Palestina Vulgaris,* and up for sale were a transistor radio in the shape of half a watermelon, with big black seeds; a red balloon in the shape of a VW car; a stuffed eagle; a box of Swiss Alps Silvana chocolates (which tasted more like soap from Nablus); a Henry the Eighth embroidered tableau; a highly decorated French-style vase; two Italian baroque angel statues; a mirror with a seashell frame; someone's mother's wedding dress; a set of plastic teacups; a heavy sealed glass box filled with blue seawater and two small floating boats; an electric fountain with pink balls that bobbed up and down when you plugged it in. But nothing, nothing, could beat my electric Mecca tableau.

As the evening went on, and the auction became more and more hilarious, I started to discover my strong attachment to my Mecca tableau. All of a sudden I started to have second thoughts about having it auctioned. I felt terrible at the thought of losing it. As Fateh started the countdown, I felt the urge to retrieve it. How could I possibly lose the Mecca tableau, which was an integral part of our neighborhood, of the al-Irsal "The Bold and Not-So-Beautiful" soap opera?

But it was too late: Emma Playfair, the director of Al-Haq Human Rights Organization, had already taken possession of the tableau, by bidding the highest possible price, some two hundred dollars, for Mecca.

With tears welling up in my eyes, I walked towards Emma, gave her a big hug, congratulated her on her latest acquisition, looked closely at what was once my tableau and discreetly said farewell to my Mecca. Without realizing the state I was in, Emma hugged me back and laughed, asking, "Is this your Mecca?" I nodded sadly.

It was the *Palestina Vulgaris* objects that got Roger out on bail. And I was happy to know that my Mecca played an important part in his temporary release.

Perhaps that was, from the very beginning, meant to be its role. In spite of Mecca's blessings and the great fun we had that night, my paranoia of the year before took control of me once again.

That very night I lost sleep worrying about Emma. What if Mecca was really bugged? Now Mossad would be spying on Emma's and Al-Haq Human Rights activities.

It was seven o'clock in the morning when I called Emma.

"Sorry, Emma, did I wake you up?" Of course I had.

"No, it is all right, Suad, what is it?" she said in her upper-class English stutter.

"Mecca, Emma," I said.

"What Mecca? Oh, yes, the Mecca tableau—what about it?" she inquired, like all good lawyers.

I felt too scared and paranoid to reveal the espionage

story on the telephone. Of course, telephones were bugged as well.

"Emma, can I come see you this morning? I urgently need to talk to you," I said in total confusion.

"Fine, why don't you come Wednesday?"

"Wednesday is too far away, it is quite urgent," I replied in a panic.

"What is today? Isn't it Tuesday?" she inquired.

"Yes, but I think it is extremely urgent. I'll come and see you this morning."

"All right, see you soon." Emma hung up and went straight back to bed, probably while uttering some polite English curse.

I tried hard to choose my words as I climbed the four flights of stairs to Emma's office. No words seemed to be suitable.

"Emma, you know how the Occupation makes us hallucinate sometimes?"

"Yes, of course I do," she assured me.

"I think the Mecca tableau you acquired at Roger's auction is bugged by Mossad," I said.

"Isn't it yours, Suad? How can it be bugged?" Emma's friendly tone was changing. She had a funny expression on her face.

Oh, what a long story. I was certainly not ready for her questions.

"Where is it?" I asked.

"At home," she replied, adding, "in my bedroom."

"Emma, *please* get rid of it immediately, OK?" I said, and walked out of her office.

I felt utterly ridiculous as I came down the steps of Al-Haq.

As I drove my car away, I could see Emma running hurriedly towards her house.

9

A Dog's Life

1987–95

It was one of those rare moments when I could easily have killed someone.

But to kill Dr. Hisham, the only vet in Ramallah (probably the only one in the whole district), would have been a national scandal. It probably would have caused a rural uproar, perhaps not one as important as the renowned 1834 Peasant Revolution against Ibrahim Pasha (the son of Mohammad Ali Pasha, the ruler of Egypt).

It all started in the peaceful town of Jericho, where Salim and I spent most of our weekends away from troubled Ramallah during the 1987 uprising.

We were driving along Khidaiwi Street (I wonder if the name has any connection with the Egyptian Khidaiwis, the descendants of Mohammad Ali Pasha) when I glimpsed two puppies cuddled up in a ditch at the side of the road. I quickly stopped the car and rushed out towards them. One was dark and one blond, and they were sitting on top of one another, keeping each other warm, in the already very warm town of Jericho. I held one in each hand and, with great excitement, looked at Salim. With a very worried expression, he looked me straight in the eye and said firmly, "NO."

"Poor little things—sooner or later they'll be run over by a car," I replied.

"No, they won't," insisted Salim.

"Look at them, they are so absolutely cute," I said as they dangled with their soft tummies exposed.

"I know," Salim replied, looking away from them.

"Why not, then?" I insisted.

"Who is going to take care of them?" asked Salim.

"I will, of course," I said joyfully, seeing that I was starting to win the case.

"You're busy and traveling most of the time. Dogs are worse than babies, they need constant attention . . . and affection," he added.

Oh, God, how this argument reminded me of the many arguments Salim and I had had over having or not having children.

But this time I was not willing to compromise.

It was heartbreaking to make *the choice*. There was no way I could have convinced Salim to adopt both puppies.

The dark brown puppy was left behind, and 'Antar the blond (of course) accompanied us home to Ramallah. The joy and excitement over acquiring 'Antar was for a long time mixed with a lot of guilt. Perhaps that's why 'Antar behaved the way he did. He probably never forgave me for separating him from his brother (or sister).

"You can tell how big a dog will grow up to be by the size of his paws," said a friend of mine as he held two of 'Antar's huge paws. That was not reassuring, as 'Antar's paws were one-third of his size. He also told me that I should change the name ('Antar bin Shaddad, a classical poet hero in Arabic literature, was known for his chivalry and heroic military deeds—in other words, a symbol of machismo), as 'Antar turned out to be a she. But it was too late.

As a matter of fact, for years we continued to treat 'Antar as a he.

"Is four in the afternoon a good time? I'll be there," said Dr. Hisham when I had explained to him 'Antar's need for an anti-rabies vaccine.

It was four o'clock sharp when vet Hisham rang the bell. I quickly opened the door and ushered him into the sitting room. There followed half an hour of typical Palestinian small talk: complaints about the terrible political situation, how selfish Palestinians had become, especially the younger generation, and about the lack of vision (except, of course, for Dr. Hisham and me) in the whole area.

Another quarter hour was spent bragging about Dr. Hisham's success stories: saving the sheep of Abu el-'Abed in the village of Surda, and the newly born twin cows in the village of 'Atarah (I had absolutely no idea how many cows are born at a time and did not dare ask), and Abu Nizar's sick horse, which Dr. Hisham brought back to life after Dr. Khaldun, from Nablus, told the owner that his five-thousand-dollar animal could not be saved.

I was quite reassured by his successes, but I also took note that none of them involved a dog.

"Dr. Hisham, I need you to give 'Antar an anti-rabies vaccine," I found myself interrupting.

"Yes, of course," he replied, suddenly recognizing my growing impatience.

"What breed is 'Antar?" asked Dr. Hisham authoritatively as he sipped his coffee.

"Ahh . . . breed . . . mmmmm . . . I am not so sure he has a breed. Can one consider a *baladi** dog a breed?" I mumbled apologetically.

To me he is 'Antar, a lovely, mischievous, rambunctious puppy.

As Dr. Hisham stared at me, I thought to myself, Why can't a *baladi* dog be a breed? "Never mind, Doctor, can I bring 'Antar in? Or shall we go out to the garden?" I was trying to rekindle Dr. Hisham's interest in the mission he had come for.

"Doesn't matter—bring him in," he replied.

In no time 'Antar was all over the place. After knocking down the tray with his long wagging tail, and splashing coffee all over the place, he rolled over on his back and waited to be patted on his very round tummy. *Typical* 'Antar, I thought to myself.

I could see Dr. Hisham looking at 'Antar's genitals.

---

* *Baladi* in Arabic means both indigenous and also vulgar.

" 'Antar is a bitch," said Dr. Hisham with great disappointment.

"You mean she is a female," I tried to correct him.

"That's what I meant," said Dr. Hisham.

"So . . . ?" I said in an irritated, high-pitched voice.

"Do you really want to waste a thirty-dollar vaccine on a *baladi* bitch?"

"I can't believe this, Dr. Hisham," I said, my anger mounting.

I kept quiet, amazed at how defending a female dog had aroused in me national, feminist and pro–animal rights emotions.

As Dr. Hisham bent down to give 'Antar her vaccine, I was on the verge of breaking the tip of another rabies vaccine and sticking it in his big, protruding backside.

A Few Years Later

It was almost 10:30 at night when I heard squeaking sounds outside. I opened the garden door, and immediately jumped back as a tiny black creature came running in. In no time, it disappeared behind the many plant pots in the front veranda. I switched on the light, and cautiously started looking behind every pot. It was not long before I spotted two huge, bat-like ears stuck on a tiny little black puppy. I stretched out my slightly trembling hand to pick up an even more trembling puppy. She was the size of my palm.

It took only a few hours for Nura and me to become forever inseparable. She became my tiny, nervous shadow. Nura, who grew to be a little bit bigger than my two palms, still accompanies me everywhere: to work, to construction sites, to my mother-in-law's house and to some but not all of my friends' houses.

Soon I had a huge collection of books on dogs: *All You Want to Know About Your Dog, Admit Sleeping with Your Dog, Loving Your Dog More than Your Husband, Can My Dog Become My Heir?, Cheating on Your Dog, What Breed Is Your Dog?* My latest book was *Growing Up with a Lesbian Master*.

I also subscribed to *Bitch* magazine.

Unlike the late 'Antar, Nura was obviously of a very special breed: a toy Manchester terrier. Reading and learning so much about Nura's special breed obviously did not change the one reality on the ground: Nura still needed the antirabies vaccine and there was no one else except Dr. Hisham who could give it to her. Because he was so openly sexist and undoubtedly racist, I had taken a decision not to deal with Dr. Hisham ever again.

After a few months of not knowing what to do, I had to make up my mind. I did not know which was more difficult: to end my boycott of the sexist Dr. Hisham, or to start dealing with an Israeli vet—probably racist against Arabs but not dogs—located in 'Atarut, an Israeli industrial zone (illegal Jewish settlement) built on Palestinian lands on the Ramallah–Jerusalem road. The Society for the Prevention of Cruelty to Animals was located just a half mile or so away from the Jerusalem checkpoint established in March 1992, at a time when the Palestinian-Israeli peace talks were taking place in Washington, D.C.

"She is a *toy Manchester terrier*," I bragged to Dr. Tamar, an Israeli veteran with an English accent.

"She is absolutely gorgeous; what is her name?" asked Dr. Tamar as she cuddled Nura.

"Nura," I said proudly.

"And yours?"

"Suad."

"Isn't she absolutely cute?" I said, trying to act as calmly as possible despite feeling nervous that someone I knew would see me sneaking into 'Atarut's Society for the Prevention of Cruelty to Animals. Looking at the sign, I was relieved that Arabs were not considered animals.

"Let's see now, we need to check her eyes, her ears, and her tiny teeth, and then give her the rabies, flu and cocktail vaccines," said Dr. Tamar as she placed Nura on a special operation table in the middle of her clinic.

"A nonalcoholic cocktail, I hope," I joked nervously.

"What about her blood pressure and diabetes?" I added.

Dr. Tamar totally ignored my remarks and walked out of her office. Maybe I was stupid to make such silly remarks, but I wanted to release some of the tension I was feeling.

It was not long before Dr. Tamar came back empty-handed.

"Suan, we seem to have a little problem here," she said in her rather serious English accent.

"What is it, Doctor?" Wanting to know what the problem was, I did not correct my name.

"Did you say Nura lives in Ramallah?" she asked.

"Yes, with me of course," I answered nervously.

"But the Jerusalem municipality vaccines are only for Jerusalem dogs."

"But you know it is illegal for us to live in Jerusalem, Doctor, as we have Ramallah IDs," I said, interrupting Dr. Tamar in a panic.

"No need to change residency. Would you be willing to pay for the vaccine?" she asked.

"*Of course* I would," I said, enthusiastically taking all the money out of my purse.

"A hundred and twenty shekels," she said, and I handed her the money. She took it and walked out of her office again.

I cuddled the trembling Nura and collapsed onto a chair next to the window. I looked at the surprising number of Palestinian women and men who had come in with their dogs and cats to seek vet Tamar's help. I wondered if they were also running away from Dr. Hisham. They all looked much more relaxed and self-assured than I did.

"We still seem to have a little problem here," I heard Dr. Tamar say before I even saw her.

"What is it?" I asked, nervously standing up.

"Well, this certificate is issued by Jerusalem municipality, and I am not sure whether it is recognized by the newly established Palestinian National Authority in Ramallah."

She must be kidding, I thought to myself, but unfortunately Dr. Tamar looked damn serious (at that time people were still taking the Oslo Agreement seriously).

Not knowing what to make of Dr. Tamar's English seriousness, I could not help laughing.

"Don't worry, Dr. Tamar. It would be good enough if the Palestinian National Authority recognized its own certificates, let alone Arab dogs holding Jerusalem certificates."

I jealously watched Dr. Tamar filling in Nura's yellow and black Jerusalem passport.

First name, name of father, name of mother, age, own breed, breed of father and mother, a list of vaccine types, date of injection, date of next injection, remarks, doctor's name and, lastly, owner's name.

"Do you have a photograph?"

"My photograph? Or Nura's?" I was hoping it would work.

"Nura's," answered Dr. Tamar.

Neither Nura nor Dr. Tamar realized how damn serious I was about replacing Nura's photograph with mine. I don't think either of them knew how difficult or impossible it is for Palestinians to acquire a Jerusalem ID, let alone a Jerusalem *passport*. I was thinking of my Jerusalemite friend Nazmi Jubeh, whose wife, Haifa, had spent sixteen years waiting for her Jerusalem ID.

I'd definitely have to hide Nura's passport from Samir Hulieleh, who after twenty-four years of marriage to Sawsan, a Jerusalemite, had not yet succeeded in getting a Jerusalem ID.

I did not want to think about adorable little Yasmin, Sawsan and Samir's only child. The Israelis would not give her a Jerusalem ID because her father had a Palestinian Ramallah ID, and the Palestinian Authority would not give her a Palestinian ID because her mother had an Israeli Jerusalem ID.

If Jewish and Arab traditions were respected, Yasmin should have two identity cards, one after her mother and one after her father. But she has none.

I was also thinking of my dear friend 'Attallah Kuttab, who had recently lost his Jerusalem ID because he married Ebba, who is German. I was thinking of the tens of thousands of Palestinians who have lost their Jerusalem IDs, and the many others who have been waiting in vain for years to acquire a Jerusalem ID.

And here was little Nura with a Jerusalem passport.

"Lucky you, baby." I picked her up and gave her a big kiss.

"Don't lose it. Take it with you when you travel abroad."

"You mean the *passport*?" I was just checking.

"Yes," Dr. Tamar replied.

Both Nura and Dr. Tamar gave me a strange look, as neither of them was that political. It drove me crazy how both took being a Jerusalemite for granted. I walked out, carrying tiny Nura in my left hand and her passport carefully in my right.

"You know what, Nura? This document will get you through the checkpoint into Jerusalem while I and my car need two different permits to get through."

Nura looked at me, slightly tilting her tiny head, wagged her long tail, put her head out of the car window and sniffed.

It was not long before I decided to make use of Nura's passport.

"Can I see your permit and the car's?" requested the soldier standing at the Jerusalem checkpoint.

"I don't have one, but I am the driver of this Jerusalem dog," I replied, handing the soldier Nura's passport.

"*Maze* (What)?" asked the soldier, making a funny face.

He looked pretty amused by the thought. He took Nura's passport and started flipping through it.

"I am the dog's driver. As you can see, she is from Jerusalem, and she cannot possibly drive the car or go to Jerusalem all by herself."

"And you argh hergh dghiver?" he said, rolling his *r*'s in the way that Israelis do when they speak English and dissolving into laughter.

"Yes, somebody has got to be her driver," I laughed back.

The soldier looked closely at me, patted Nura's head, which was still sticking out of the window, handed me her passport and in a loud voice said: "*SA'A* . . . Go."

I pressed my foot on the accelerator, Nura stuck half of her tiny body out of the window, and to Jerusalem we both flew.

All it takes is a bit of humor, I thought to myself as Nura and I passed the same soldier when we drove back to Ramallah that same afternoon.

10

Diala's First Encounter

August 1992

It was a boiling hot summer day. I was baking in the heat wave as I drove to pick up my eighteen-year-old niece, Diala, who had just arrived in Jerusalem.

It must have been those endearing pink pajamas of hers that created the strong, lifelong bond between Diala and me. I still vividly remember my stroll along al-Hamra, then the most fashionable street in Beirut. It was a lovely April day. With great excitement, I told the shopkeeper at al-Zahhar's baby shop that I wanted some Very Special Pajamas for my newborn niece (hoping she would grow up to adore sleeping, just like her auntie). With a grumpy face he looked at me and handed me the pajamas.

"These are very special. We sell at least ten pairs a day."

I wanted to explain to him that Diala was truly special. She was the family's first grandchild and probably the last. I wanted to tell him that even though there were three sisters and one brother, none except for Arwa, Diala's mother, had a child. My sister 'Anan had married twice with no children. I, so far, had married once, with no children; Ayman, my only brother, never got married, hence no children. I wanted to share all of this with him, so he might understand how special Diala was, but I was afraid to reveal how terrified we all were to produce children who might resemble us.

OK, the pajamas may have not been that special, but Diala definitely was.

I was in seventh heaven. At last I had managed to get a permit to have one of my family members living in Amman, Damascus or Beirut visit me in Ramallah. But getting the visitor's permit at the Israeli Civil Administration is one thing; helping relatives overcome their fears in order to make the trip is another.

My mother, who is Syrian, had adopted President Assad's political stand: "NO to normalization with Israel."

"For God's sake, Mother, I am your daughter, visiting me in Ramallah is not normalization with Israel."

"*Habibti* Susu (My beloved Susu), I don't need to tell you how much I would love to visit you and Salim in Ramallah. Do you know what it means for a mother not to see her daughter's home after eight years of marriage?" my mother said as tears welled in her greyish-green eyes. The expression on her face forced me to drop the subject instantly.

I was not sure which was more difficult: for my mother to drop her ideological stand, or for the Israeli military governor of Ramallah to approve her visitor's permit. Perhaps her rejection was in anticipation of his refusal.

She was a proud woman, after all.

Now that Diala had made it, I was more hopeful that next summer, I could get my mother a visitor's permit. Rain or shine, I would dedicate a few weeks of my time to standing in these unbearable crowds in front of the military compound.

With my right arm across my chest and my left steering the car, I found myself pledging at the top of my voice: "Mother, I promise, next year in Jerusalem."

Opposite Damascus Gate stood voluptuous Diala, colorful as ever, her striking red skirt topped with an orange low-cut T-shirt. Green and yellow beaded jewelry, designed and made by her, added to her joyful look and demonstrated her artistic talents. She was nervously moving her beautifully shaped head in all directions, trying to absorb decades of her nostalgic mother's descriptions, her deceased grandfather's deprivations and her unfulfilled grandma's aspirations.

"Hi, beautiful, it takes much longer to grasp the situation," I told her jokingly, as our laughter and tears mingled.

"Ahhhhhhhhh, I am in Jerusalem. I just can't believe it!" came her excited teenage scream.

As I opened the trunk to throw in Diala's bag, I could see the piercing dark eyes of young men staring at us (her not-so-modest clothes did not help).

I parked the car in al-Musrarah, near the Arab laborers' market. This is where young men appeared every morning, as early as five o'clock, in the hope of being picked up by an Israeli employee. When the car of an Israeli slowed down, a crowd of workers rushed to it. In no time they surrounded it, opened the three passenger doors while it was still in motion, and pushing fiercely with their elbows, four made it into the car. Because the fight demonstrated the survival of the fittest, the Israeli, realizing he had got the strongest men, drove away.

Even though it was already noon, many men were still waiting to be picked up. While some were staring, stunned, at my beloved niece, an Israeli car appeared behind their backs, picked up four and left. They realized they had missed their very last opportunity, and we could hear the fight and the commotion as we drove away.

"Well, well, well, at last you're here." I bent to kiss her. With the kiss the car swayed.

"Please, *Khalto,* I love Jerusalem but I don't want to die in Jerusalem."

"Not even for Jerusalem," I added.

"OK, let's see what to show you," I said to Diala as she bounced restlessly in the car seat.

"Dome of the Rock as seen from the Mount of Olives," I said firmly.

That would be quite impressive, I thought.

I drove the car through al-Musrarah, through Sa'ed wa Said, through Sheikh Jarrah, through Wadi el-Juz, through al-Sowanneh, *not* through the Hebrew University, *not* through the French Hill and *not* through Saddiq Shimun in the Sheikh Jarrah neighborhood.

It was too early to depress her, I thought to myself.

"This is the Ghosheh family house where your grandparents lived before 1948," I said to Diala as we drove past the beautiful stone house by the Mount Scopus Hotel.

"This is where they lived after 1948," I added as I pointed out the Turkish Consulate in the Sheik Jarrah neighborhood.

We kept driving.

Soon we were standing on the Mount of Olives panoramic esplanade, overlooking the most overwhelming and overpowering view of Jerusalem.

"Boy. Fabulous, really cool," Diala yelled, giving me a big hug.

I must admit, describing the Dome of the Rock as "cool" was rather irritating. But I decided it was too early for me to be the politically correct aunt.

I was intentionally avoiding pointing out Jewish landmarks or Israeli settlements. I really wanted her to see how Arab East Jerusalem still existed, in the hope of convincing more of my family members to visit me. But it was not that easy.

"Oh, what a lovely hotel!" Diala said as we passed the Hyatt Regency.

"If you knew that the Israelis confiscated Raja Shehadeh's father's land to build this bloody hotel, you would not say it was lovely." The words just flew out of my mouth.

I knew I should not be harsh on her. The Israelis are very skilled at not leaving any traces showing that others were living on this land not so long ago.

Our conversation ground to a halt as we both saw a middle-aged man standing almost in the middle of the road, next to the open door of his car. Bent half over, with one hand on his chest, and the other waving, he was screaming for help.

I immediately stopped the car, jumped out and ran to him.

"What is it?" I inquired in English.

"I think I'm having a heart attack."

"Get in the car, get in the car," I yelled at the man as I helped him get in the backseat.

"Run and close his car door," I ordered Diala. She slammed it shut and came running back to the front seat.

I pressed the accelerator as hard as I could and drove the car towards Hadassah Hospital at Mount Scopus.

"Are you OK?" I asked, looking at him in the rearview mirror.

"Ah, it must be the terrible heat that caused it," he replied.

"Don't worry, just relax, we will soon be there," I assured him.

"Where?" he asked, a note of fear creeping into his voice.

"Hadassah Hospital," I answered.

What sort of a question is that? I thought to myself. The poor thing, he must have realized by now that we were Palestinians. Oh, God . . . all the more reason for him to have another heart attack. It might be fatal this time.

Diala was in total shock. She must have figured out by now that the man was an Israeli. She must have figured out why I was speaking in English. She was speechless.

I was aware how apprehensive Diala was about meeting Israelis, like most Diaspora Palestinians and Arabs. Having realized that, I had carefully worked out a way to have her meet some of my Israeli friends. I had planned to invite Judy and Ruth for dinner, but not at the beginning of her trip. I was attentive to her fears and how to slowly overcome them. I was scared of the consequences if I failed.

All of a sudden the absurdity of the situation dawned on me. What if he had a fatal heart attack in the backseat of my car?

Would the Israeli police ever believe I was just trying to help? It had happened without my giving it any thought. I simply meant to take him to hospital.

Oh, God, what a mess. What would the Israeli Army do once they found his abandoned car? There would definitely be a countrywide alert any minute now. I didn't want to think about how many young Palestinian men would be arrested as suspects due to my irresponsible, thoughtless act.

I really did not want Diala to know what kind of state I was in, or what kind of crazy thoughts were crossing my mind. I was trying hard to make it look like what it really was: the emergency of taking a sick man to the hospital. That by itself was dramatic enough.

I got my hallucinations under control and tried to start acting normally.

"You've been waiting all your life to encounter one, see how easy it is?!" I joked in Arabic with Diala, trying to release some of the tension in the front seat.

I don't think I succeeded.

There was more panic in both the front and backseats. Diala opened her already large eyes even wider, and raised her eyebrows.

In the rearview mirror, I checked on the sick man. His face was dripping with sweat, and I could see the fear on his face as he heard me speak Arabic.

"Are you OK? Hold on, we're almost there," I said, driving speedily up the hill towards the hospital.

"Are you from Betlaikhem (Bethlehem)?" he inquired wearily, in a heavy Israeli-English accent.

I wanted to lie and tell him yes, we are from the town of peace, but I did not.

I wanted to help the poor dying man hold on to one of the Israelis' comforting myths, but could not.

"Ramallah," I answered as I talked to him through the mirror.

"Ramallah?" He was totally horrified.

"Why don't you relax a bit?" I answered him. I really wanted him to just stop asking questions, as the shock might be too much for his poor heart. But he continued:

"Ramallah is a Christian town."

"Used to be," I said in a matter-of-fact tone.

"You're Christian?"

"Muslim," I replied.

There was a deadly silence in the back. I hoped it was only a figure of speech.

I did not dare look behind me.

I parked the car as close to the emergency door as possible and dashed into the hospital screaming for help. It was not long before I came running back with three emergency nurses and a trolley.

Diala stood still.

The nurses rushed to the car, got the man out of the backseat and onto the stretcher.

I was in a state of total fright. I was scared to look at him. Once I gathered my courage, I stole a quick glance; his eyes were wide open.

"There are good Palestinians after all," I heard him mumble, as they rushed him away.

Diala and I looked at one another, and I stood there praying those would not be the last words he uttered before he faced his Lord.

As we drove away, I thought of my father, who died in 1978 from a massive heart attack. He was all alone in his hotel room. I always felt terrible that he must have sought help but none arrived.

PART TWO

11

Cappuccino in Ramallah

4 *December* 2001

My husband, Salim, and I were at Mamdouh and Ohoud's for Ramadan *iftar* (evening meal). There were about fourteen of us sitting around the long dining table, which Ohoud, as was often the case, had filled with a variety of delicious foods, in addition to Ramadan's special drinks and sweets. The chat and noise was suddenly interrupted when we heard the news about the Israeli bombardment of Arafat's private helicopters and offices in Gaza. Both Maher and Mamdouh started envisaging the different scenarios of what Sharon and his government might do this evening. The scenarios varied from attacking Arafat's headquarters in Ramallah to reoccupying parts of Ramallah and al-Bireh. Salim and I looked at one another across the table, with worried minds and anxious smiles. If the first scenario turned out to be true, then my mother-in-law would be in real danger, as her house directly overlooked Arafat's headquarters. And if the second scenario turned out to be true, then our neighborhood would be occupied and the Israeli soldiers would once again be literally on our doorstep. Given the choice, which one would we choose? Of course, they both came true the morning after. We were woken at 2:30 in the morning by the sound of heavy tanks. We jumped out of bed, rushed towards our bedroom window overlooking the main street and cautiously sneaked a look through the curtains, but, soon after, we both went back to bed and fell asleep, as we had seen it all before only a few weeks previously.

Around 4:30 in the morning Salim asked me if I wanted a cappuccino; three-quarters asleep, I answered, "Well, why not?"

All of a sudden I remembered the last time the Israeli soldiers were right outside our kitchen windows. So I rushed to the kitchen and told Salim to be careful, as the cappuccino machine makes too much noise and hence may be extremely risky. Later on in the morning Salim complained that he had basically risked his life to make me the cappuccino, only to find out that I had fallen asleep again.

"Nothing changes," he complained. "Not even under occupation," he added.

At 7:40 I was woken by the first phone call, from Vanouch.

"Oh, no . . . no, I am awake," I answered apologetically, with a husky, sleepy voice, ashamed that I was still asleep even under occupation. "Yes, they came at two-thirty in the morning, we woke up to the loud noises of the military tanks, then we fell asleep and at four-thirty Salim went to make us cappuccino, and when he came back I was asleep; he later complained that he had risked his life only to find me asleep.

"Thanks, Vanouch. We will take care.

"Bye."

At 8:30, the phone rang.

"Hi, Vera.

"No, Vanouch woke me up.

"They came at two-thirty. Lots of noise, woke up, fell asleep, cappuccino, risked his life."

"No, fine.

"Thanks.

"Bye."

At 9:00.

"Hello, Gabi.

"No, no, no, Vanouch, then Vera called, fine.

"Yes, thanks, at two-thirty, cappuccino."

At 9:15.

"Hi, baby. Johnson.

"No, no, I am fully awake!

"Not at one, at two-thirty.

"No, not four, six tanks.

"Yes, cappuccino.

"Don't worry, thanks."

At 9:40.

"Oh, *marhaba hamati* (Hello, my mother-in-law), how are you?

"No, no, fine.

"No, really, everything is fine.

"The line has been busy.

"Yes, friends have been calling.

"No, no tanks, not here.

"Perhaps another al-Irsal Street.

"No, not our al-Irsal.

"Fine.

"Yes, lots of thunder last night.

"Yes, we also thought they were tanks.

"Yes, Sharon is really *majnoon* (absolutely crazy).

"We'll pass by later in the day.

"Bye."

At 10:00.

"Hi, Suha.

"You heard the news in Amman? I am really sorry you are so worried. Yes.

"Kitchen.

"Two-thirty.
"Cappuccino.
"Salim."

At 10:50.
"Hello.
"Dafna Golan, hi.
"Fine.
"Thanks.
"Would you like to hear how close?
"Listen.
"Oh, thanks, Dafna, for your lovely call."

At 11:20.
"Yes, hello, Mother.
"Occupied our neighborhood?
"Oh, no, no, far . . . far away from here.
"Yes, yes, al-Irsal Street, but not our Irsal!
"Don't worry, Mama, we are safe.
"No, Um Salim is at her house, thank God! She is safe too.
"Don't cry, Mama, we are really OK.
"Hugs and kisses, Mama.
"Yes, for sure I will come to see you in Amman for the *'Eid.*"

At 12:00.

"Rema, I am doing much better this time.

"Oh, no, we shall not leave this time.

"At two-thirty, cappuccino, fell asleep at four-thirty.

"Thanks.

"Bye."

At 12:23.

"Oh, hi, Taisir."

"Hello, Islah. Oh, it's your fiftieth birthday! How sweet."

"Hello, Janin."

"Hello, Hisham."

"Bonjour, Brigitte."

"Bonjour, Rania."

"Hello, Fida."

"*Ahlan,* Farhat."

"Hi, Najwa."

"Yes, Eman, so good to hear your voice from Canada."

The phone rang again at around 11:30 that night as I was falling asleep.

There had been fifty-three phone calls that day!

12

Our New Neighbors

5 December 2001

Just a few days before our new neighbors moved in, I was complaining to my friends Vera, who lives in al-Bireh, and Rema, who lives in a beautiful old house in the Sheikh Jarrah area of Jerusalem, how unbearable life had become in our neighborhood. Mounds of building rubble were now the main feature of the landscape, and the sidewalks only appeared now and then, making walking straight a big challenge. Dusty grey had become the national color, while green was a rarity, fresh air was an impossibility and my list of complaints grew longer and longer as I went on "nagging" (as Salim would have said).

Our neighborhood, al-Irsal, could still be described as one of the nicer residential areas in Ramallah. It is relatively pleasant and child-friendly. It is safe for children to play in the streets, hence the dozens of them running around screaming and fighting, some playing football, little ones playing *tummayettekhbay* (hide-and-seek), a few riding bicycles.

Our neighborhood is like any other neighborhood. It looks normal and ordinary, but it has a lot to offer in terms of gossip and family scandals, if one is interested, or, more important, has the time to spend with the neighbors. Nowadays, I hardly visit any of the neighbors, but, like most, I manage to keep closely in touch with the neighborhood gossip: affairs, collaborators, drugs, marital discord. Sami and Wafa were a married couple who were always fighting and, as a result, their extended families got involved, and even got into physical fights. I remember, a few years ago, there was a bang at the door, and when Salim opened it, there was Fahmi, the neighbors' son, breathless, calling on "*ammo* Salim" to join in a fight, as the *khalayleh** families of the bride were attacking to save their daughter. A big fight took place in the neighborhood and a few people were injured. A week or two later, Sami and Wafa were back together, happily married and producing more and more bambinos, but of course we remained the neighbors who betrayed them by not joining the fight. Both Salim and I have learned the hard way. I try to follow, closely, from a distance, the gossip and scandals of our neighborhood, but never get directly involved, as it can sometimes get messy. And it did more than once. I had learned the hard way from Um Zahi and Rami's soap opera.

Every morning, we get up at exactly eight o'clock to the sound of the Palestinian national anthem—*Bilaadi, bilaaaadi, bilaaaaadi ya ardi ya ardah eljudud*—coming from the shrieking voices of the little schoolgirls up the road. Even if these

* Slang for people from Hebron.

shrieking voices did not get us up, the ice cream kids (whose father makes and sells ice cream) would be sure we got up. They live across the road from our house, and there are about a dozen of them, ranging in age from two to six. (Don't ask me how, but believe me, it's true.) Since they live in a two-room house, they are always running around in the street near their ill-defined front yard. My biggest obsession and nightmare is that I might run one over someday, *la samah ellah* (God forbid). The only reassuring thing is that they are so noisy that if you happen not to see them, you will definitely hear them. They drive the wife of the *mukhtar* crazy by continually stepping on her vegetable garden.

The *mukhtar*'s wife is by definition a good gardener, a peasant woman originally from the village of Lifta. She and her older husband live in a nice old two-story stone house, with a lovely back garden with vineyards and sunflowers. I often admire her laundry line, spread with beautifully embroidered traditional dresses in lovely bright colors.

Abu Nader, the little shopkeeper up the road, also has ten little ones. But in this case, their ages range from two years to twenty. Hence only five or six are seen playing and screaming up the road from us. Sari, Basil, Abudeh, Jamal and Dodo are the next-door neighbor's kids. They are our local football team; they play right in front of our veranda, and manage to break our windows an average of once a month. . . . Goal! they scream.

The honking of cars strangled at the Birzeit Road checkpoint only adds flavor to a neighborhood that has lost its serenity but not its liveliness.

One of the sadder cases in our neighborhood is that of Um Maher. She lives directly behind our house, and we share a garden wall. In addition to her quite normal kids, Um Maher has two mentally handicapped boys, Maher, her eldest son, and Saher, and she spends most of her time taking care of them. She often cries out of frustration and sadness. From our bedroom, every morning I see Um Maher, with the help of her Sri Lankan maid, carry the two chairs and the two boys, now more like men, out to the garden and leave them out to get a little bit of sun and fresh air. I often hear the two boys mumbling as I work at my computer.

In the middle of last night, new neighbors moved into our neighborhood. In spite of its being early on a Ramadan day (when people get up late), they were extremely loud, inconsiderate and noisy. They were rather a big crowd, moving about in huge and environmentally unfriendly vehicles. Some just camped in the empty lot in front of our house, next to the clothesline of the *mukhtar*'s wife, a few feet away from the ice cream shop and just opposite us. The others arrived in a bulldozerlike vehicle whose vibrations traveled through the ground and could be felt under our feet. They stopped and swiftly seemed to settle outside the building opposite the house of Um Maher and across from our kitchen window. We all watched them silently from behind our closed windows, making sure we didn't make any noise. We all kept shifting from one room to the other, watching their moves closely. Later that night, with spinning heads, we all sort of fell asleep.

When we woke up, there was a long silence, a deadly silence, a fearful silence, a silence that made us realize that the new neighbors were alien bodies. They were creatures who made the ice cream children melt, and who brought with them a silence that stopped the mumblings of Maher and Saher, a silence that brought more tears to Um Maher, a silence that froze the shredded glass of our veranda, and stilled the honking of the cars at the Birzeit roadblock.

The only sound violating this deadly silence was the ghastly voice coming from the loudspeaker: *"Mamnou' al-tajawol khkhatta esharen akhar* (A curfew is declared)."

Oh, how I missed the voices shrieking, *"Bilaaaaaaadi!"*

13

Ramallah Under Curfew

29 March–1 May 2002

I   The Balcony

The Second Lifting of the Curfew
5 April 2002

Today was the eighth day of the Israeli reoccupation of the already Occupied Territories. This was the second time they had lifted the curfew since the military incursions started on 29 March 2002.

During the Gulf War in 1991, the Israeli Army kept more than two million Palestinians under curfew for forty-two days, in anticipation of the unknown or, as the Israeli Army claimed then, for "security" reasons. Every few days they would lift the curfew for "humane" reasons, so that civilians could go out to buy food and medicine. Ramallah would become an absolutely frantic town, with everyone running like crazy to do their shopping before the three-hour respite was over. Every now and then, I used to refuse to leave the house, in defiance of Israel's decision: "Now you can come out of your houses and run like crazy as we watch you, while pointing our guns at you just in case."

The first time they lifted this curfew, on 2 April, I learned about the respite from the TV after it was over. None of my friends could reach me, as telephone lines had been cut in our neighborhood, which was only a half mile or so away from President Arafat's besieged compound. At least we had electricity, thank God. The area immediately around Arafat, where my ninety-one-year-old mother-in-law, Um Salim, lived, had no electricity, telephones or water, as I learned from her when I first saw her twelve days later.

I felt angry and frustrated as I was waiting for an opportunity to go and check on Um Salim and Zakiyyeh, her helper. I wanted to try to reach them and see how they were doing, and now I'd have to wait for the next lifting of the curfew. As it turned out, my mother-in-law was anxiously waiting for me to appear to take her and Zakiyyeh away from their house, which was at the front line. She waited and waited until she heard the Israeli soldiers shouting *mamnu il tajawwul*, announcing the end of the lifting. Three hours of waiting left my mother-in-law and Zakiyyeh in despair. Um Salim cried as Zakiyyeh tried to comfort her. Exhausted, they both fell asleep at six, I was later told.

Three days later the mobile phone, which Sari, my thirteen-year-old neighbor, had given me, rang. It was Vera: "*Yalla,* Suad, get ready. They are going to lift the curfew in fifteen minutes, Tania and I will come with you to fetch Tante Mary (Um Salim)." I drove my car along the Nablus road, which had been dug up by the Israeli tanks and bulldozers. The road looked like a route to hell. It was so dusty from all the cars trying to find their way through the ditches and rubble that I could hardly see where I was going. It took me half an hour to get to Vera's, as most of the other roads were also either blocked with rubble or pitted with big holes. Three times, I found myself face-to-face with the Israeli tanks. I shuddered with fear and turned back, as many other cars were doing, causing traffic jams. Ramallah and al-Bireh looked like a war zone. Electricity poles were upside down, there were dozens of flattened cars scattered on the road and glass and debris were everywhere. Through the mazelike town, I finally managed to get to Vera's. There, we hugged, cried and talked all at the same time. At that very moment, Nabil and Vanouch appeared. Again we hugged one another and the first thing Vanouch asked me was, "Is it true the Israeli Army stormed your organization, Riwaq?"* I looked at her and said, "Oh! No, who told you that?" She said, "Hala's sister saw Israeli tanks in the vicinity of your office two days ago but she was not sure." Oh, God, no. But I had to refocus on my main mission, which was to go and see my mother-in-law. I looked at Vera and said, "*Yalla,* Vera and Tania, let's go." We got in the car. Just next to Vera's house were three cars, two totally flattened and a third smashed and used to barricade the road. I reversed the car, again in the middle of the road, and we drove past Islah's house. I stopped the car and ran

* The Center for Architectural Conservation.

up to it. I opened the door and there stood Islah. She is usually bubbly and full of energy, but now she looked like a ghost—she was pale, with a dazed expression. We hugged and cried. "Please, Suad, come and stay with us, don't stay alone. Those bastards are doing house-to-house searches. They are cruel. They blow open doors instead of ringing the doorbell, Suad, they are arresting people, stealing things, vandalizing homes. Please, Suad, come and stay with us," Islah said hysterically.

"OK, Islah, we will discuss it when I come back later." She looked through her purse and handed me her mobile phone, saying, "Please at least keep this with you." I took her mobile only to comfort her and said, "Islah, I am going to see Um Salim and will be back soon. Do you need anything?" "Yes," she replied, "we ran out of butane gas for the stove. Come back with your car and let's try to get a bottle." "Sure," I said, and went running back to the car. We drove a few hundred feet up the road, which was blocked. I took a left but that road was also blocked. I reversed and went right. Blocked again. We parked the car and walked up the hill towards Um Salim's house.

As we turned the corner we came face-to-face with an Israeli tank and a military jeep. We froze, looked at one another and wondered what would be next. I said helplessly, "Fuck you, you bastards." Tania said, "Hell, I am going to walk through the backyards behind the house." Both Vera and I said, "No, Tania, it's too dangerous." We stood there just until Vera said, "*Khalas yikhrub beithum* (Damn it, enough). I am going to walk towards the tank and jeep and explain to them that we are trying to check on my ninety-one-year-old auntie." Tania walked second in line and I followed slowly behind. My heart sank thinking of the woman whom the Israelis shot and killed two days before as she was leaving Ramallah hospital. I was also mumbling to myself, "Come on, Suad, have some courage; it's true Um Salim is Tania and Vera's aunt, but she is also your mother-in-law, *hamati*!" I was ashamed of myself for being third in line.

As all of this was racing through my mind, we heard the Israeli soldiers shouting through their loudspeakers in distorted Arabic, "*Eghrja* (Go back)!" The three of us froze and together turned away from the soldiers, with our backs to them. I was in front this time. We dragged our feet and tried to think of an alternative strategy to get to Tante Mary/Um Salim. I thought perhaps I should use telepathy to get Zakiyyeh to come out to the back balcony, which was facing us, and only some six hundred feet away. As I was concentrating, I heard Tania's operatic voice saying, "Zakiyyeh . . . Zakiyyeh . . . Zakiyyeh." Vera and I joined in and started shouting "Zakiyyeh." And just when we were about to give up, Zakiyyeh appeared on the balcony. We were so excited and happy, we almost started jumping.

"*Keefek* Zakiyyeh, *keef* Um Salim? *Wheenha?* (How are you, Zakiyyeh, how is Um Salim? Where is she?)" Zakiyyeh kept waving her hand, but we were not sure if she heard us. After a few minutes of waving Zakiyyeh turned her back to us and walked away. We waited anxiously and a few minutes later Um Salim appeared, together with Zakiyyeh. We all started shouting again, "Um Salim, Tante Mary, *keefek?*" We got no reply, as Zakiyyeh was too busy pointing towards us, trying to explain to Um Salim, who cannot see very far. Um Salim waited outside for a few minutes and then walked back inside. With tears in our eyes we also walked away, not knowing whether we had succeeded in comforting her or only made her more anxious about her siege.

We spent the next two hours running around trying to buy a few food items. Buying bread alone took one and a half hours of waiting in the overcrowded al-Sha'b bakery. It was almost four, the end of the lifting of the curfew. As the streets became slowly deserted, I gave Tania and Vera a ride home, and then drove back home myself, exhausted, dusty, rusty and frustrated. I was ready to hit the sack.

As I was falling asleep, I remembered, Oh, God, Islah has no gas. And what about Riwaq!

II   The Purple Dress

The Third Lifting of the Curfew
8 April 2002

At 12:30 in the morning, the phone rang.

"Yes, Vera, I heard they are lifting the curfew, and the first thing I want to do is try again to reach Um Salim."

"OK, good luck."

I parked my car a few feet away from the tanks standing immediately outside my mother-in-law's house. From a distance, I could see Eman, her neighbor. I shouted, "Eman, what do you think? Can I get to her?" "Come from behind," she screamed back.

I tried to find my way through an empty lot behind Eman's, just looking at the ground and hoping none of the Israeli soldiers would see me or shoot at me. I walked fast and fairly steadily. The few hundred feet felt more like a few hundred miles. I got to Eman's, climbed her garden wall and jumped. I walked through her garden and climbed another wall, this one higher. On the other side of the wall, I could see Sahar and Jad, my mother-in-law's neighbors. I felt a big sense of relief. "Hi, Sahar!" I shouted excitedly. "Hello, Suad," she answered back in an exhausted, quiet voice. Jad, her husband, and Zuheir, the other neighbor, helped me jump down. I twisted my ankle. I gazed at their faces—they all had dark lines around their eyes, Jad's and Zuheir's beards were unshaved, and they looked miserable. They were whispering, as the Israeli soldiers were just around the corner. It seemed that the Israelis had also come through the back way. I learned from them that they had managed to get their little ones and wives out of the building. "You must get your mother-in-law out, *haram* (have pity)," they said. "It has been hell here—there have been no water, no electricity and no telephones for twelve consecutive days now. The shelling was terrifying. Just take her away." I felt so guilty and tried to explain to them that I had been trying but the army turned me back. "Yes, we know," they replied. I left them and went upstairs through piles of garbage bags. As I approached the door, my mother-in-law appeared. The minute she saw me she started crying, "Where the hell were you? I have been waiting for you. They lifted the curfew twice and I waited for you, but you didn't come. We have had no electricity, no water, no telephone, shelling day and night, the food in the fridge is all rotten. All the neighbors ran away and there is only Um Jamil and Zakiyyeh here, three helpless women. . . . I am coming with you." "Of course," I said, "that's why I'm here now, to take you away with me. . . . OK, Mother, let's get out of here as soon as possible. The army is surrounding the building and we have to move quickly."

"But what should I take with me?"

"Just get your medicine, your money and your jewelry," I said firmly.

"What shall I wear?"

"Don't change. Come as you are. Just get some extra clothing."

"What shall I take?" She was totally confused and I was getting nervous.

It seemed we'd never get out of there.

"Shall I bring my purple dress?" she inquired.

"Fine, yes, purple is nice."

"But where is it?"

"In your closet, isn't it?"

"Yes, I think so." She opened her cupboard.

"Can't find it."

I reached for it.

"Here it is," I said.

"Oh, God, I can't seem to find anything anymore."

"It's OK, Um Salim, we are not going to any parties. Anything will do—just be quick, we have to get out of here as quickly as possible."

"Do you think yellow goes with purple?"

"Yes, yellow is very nice with purple, all colors are nice with purple."

"But I cannot find my yellow blouse."

"Never mind, get any color of blouse," I said, losing my patience. "Listen, Mother, we need to get out of here as quickly as possible. I sneaked in from the back. Your area is a closed military zone and we are not safe here, we have to get out."

It suddenly occurred to me: God, how am I going to get her to jump over both walls? Well, we'd cross that bridge when we came to it, if we ever came to it. I started again to persuade Um Salim to hurry.

"Come on, Mother, any clothes will do. Just take something with you."

"Shall I take winter or summer clothes? You know I put away all my summer clothes."

"OK, then get winter clothes."

"But it may get warm soon, it is already mid-April."

I suddenly realized we were not getting anywhere, so I started grabbing whatever was at hand and shoving it in a bag. Um Salim got nervous and upset.

"No, not that way," she objected to my mishandling of her clothing.

"Oh, God, I can't find anything anymore," she added.

"Get your money and jewelry out."

"Right. . . . Where did I put it? Yes, there." She opened the other cupboard. "Here, I think." She looked through piles of things and through many pockets.

"Never mind, just leave it. We'll come back soon and get it."

"That's what we said in 1948 when we left our house in Jaffa; it was May then."

Oh, God . . . her words left me speechless.

I stood still and cried.

I decided to let her take her time, even if we both got stuck here forever. I was left with no energy.

"Here." She handed me her money and jewelry.

"Come on, let's go, Suad. Shall I take some of my oil paintings with me?"

"No," I replied firmly, even though I love her paintings.

"Shall we take the lemons?"

"No."

"Shall we take the Nido (milk powder)?"

"No."

"Shall we water the plants?"

"No."

"Where is Zakiyyeh? We cannot leave without her."

"No, we cannot leave without Zakiyyeh."

"Perhaps she went to see Um Jamil, the neighbor."

I ran out, and rang the bell at Um Jamil's apartment across the hallway. I waited . . . rang again . . . no answer. I went back to Um Salim.

"Did you find her?" she inquired.

"No one is there."

"We cannot leave her behind," Um Salim said again.

"No, of course we can't."

I became totally helpless and confused. We both sat there. I ran down again and asked Zuheir, "Have you seen Zakiyyeh and Um Jamil?"

"Yes, they went out to buy some food. They ran out of food."

"Where did they go?" I asked anxiously.

"I saw them walking away an hour ago, just as you arrived. They helped one another climb over the wall. . . . I also helped push them up the wall," he said with a shy smile.

"Can you help me and my mother-in-law get up the wall, Zuheir?" I asked.

"Suad . . . you must be out of your mind!" he said, with a big exclamation mark on his face. "You expect your ninety-one-year-old mother-in-law to climb that wall?"

"Then what can I do?" I asked in desperation.

He looked more perplexed than me. "You'll have to walk with her in front of the building."

"But there are Israeli tanks and jeeps there," I answered back.

"Yes, I know."

"Then?"

"Well, that's the only way out."

"You think they will shoot at us?"

"Let's hope not," he said.

Not very reassuring, I thought.

Once again I ran up the stairs, more confused and scared than ever. But with a very confident voice I managed to say, "*Yalla*, Mother, let's go."

"Where is Zakiyyeh?"

"She went out shopping."

"So we will wait for her."

"No, I'll take you and come back for Zakiyyeh later."

"OK," she said in a resigned voice.

I grabbed her with one hand and her huge bag in the other and started walking slowly down the steps, one step at a time. "Be careful, don't step on the garbage bags."

"It stinks," she said. "Can we take the garbage bags out with us?"

"No, Mother, I am carrying too many things."

"The cleaning lady has not come lately," she complained.

We walked through Zuheir's apartment as he was cleaning out rotten food from the fridges. "We had to escape with the girls and did not have enough time to throw things away," he said apologetically.

"So, Zuheir, what shall I do?"

"Suad . . . just walk with her around the building and pray."

Would God respond to nonbelievers, I thought to myself? I started praying anyway. I took my mother-in-law tightly by the hand and started giving her instructions about each step. As I was doing so, I came face-to-face with Israeli tanks and jeeps. I couldn't and didn't want to see the faces of the soldiers inside them.

"Look at the tanks—my goodness, they're huge!" Um Salim commented.

I was breathless and kept concentrating on each of her steps. I wanted to make sure she did not fall down. We were both shaking, one out of old age and one out of failing courage.

We walked in the middle of the road, as the sidewalks had been totally ripped up.

"Why are the electricity poles in the way?" Um Salim inquired.

"Why are the cars flattened?

"Why are we walking in the middle of the road?

"Why . . . ?

"Why . . . ?

"I'm getting tired—is the car far away?

"No, Mother, we are almost there."

I opened the car door, and not so gently pushed her into the backseat and drove away.

III   The Marmalade

7:30 *in the Morning,* 10 *April* 2002

"What a pity we did not carry the begonia pot with us that you gave me on Easter Sunday." This was the first thing my mother-in-law said to me as I got out of bed at 7:30 to open the door for Nura.

"It is OK, Um Salim, our hands were full of more important things," I answered back with half-open eyes.

"*Khsarah* (What a pity), it will die," she mumbled.

"People in Nablus and Jenin are dying under the rubble of their houses," I mumbled back quietly, so as not to depress her even more.

She went to the kitchen and started boiling the marmalade she had soaked the day before. I was listening to the BBC Radio report about Kofi Annan's request for an international protection force to be sent to the Palestinian Territories, and the need to declare the Palestinian Territories human disaster emergency areas.

"I can't find the sugar."

I got out of bed again and handed her two bags of sugar.

"Do we have enough? What if they do not lift the curfew for a few more days?"

"It is OK, just use it. We have more."

I sought refuge in my bedroom again. "Colin Powell decided not to meet with Arafat today, Wednesday, in an attempt to pressure Arafat to condemn the terrorist attacks," continued the BBC reporter.

"Oh, God, I am so tired. I don't know why I get so tired so quickly," said my ninety-one-year-old mother-in-law as she passed my bedroom door.

"I wonder why too," I mumbled back.

A few minutes later and through the half-shut door of my bedroom, I heard her moaning.

"Ah, oh, my God. *Ah ya emmi.*" I pretended not to hear.

"Ah, my God. Oh, *mamma mia,*" the moaning continued. I got out of bed and walked across the hallway towards her bedroom. She was lying in bed with her back towards me.

"What's wrong, Um Salim, are you OK?" I said tenderly as I patted her on the shoulder.

"Oh, God, I'm so tired, I don't know why. I'm not the same as I used to be."

"It is OK, Mother, none of us is OK or the same anymore," I replied.

"What will happen to the marmalade?" she asked with a worried voice.

"Don't worry about it. It was meant to keep you busy and entertain you. It was not meant to fatigue you. Just have some rest and you and the marmalade will be OK."

"But I have not had my breakfast yet."

"OK, I'll prepare it for you and bring it to you in bed."

"But now, I must have my breakfast at eight."

"*Hader* (Right away), at eight sharp." As I walked away towards the kitchen, I mumbled again in a not-so-quiet voice this time, "What a pain . . ."

"Here you are," I placed the tray on her lap in bed.

"Don't you have a bigger plate for the egg?" she inquired.

I went back to the kitchen and brought two plates in ascending size. I tried the first.

"Is this OK?"

"No."

"Is this one OK?" as I handed her the second.

"Never mind," she said.

Allah ye samhak ya Salim (Oh, God, where the hell are you, Salim?), I thought to myself.

I went to bed for the fourth time in less than half an hour. But this time, for sanity's sake, I completely shut the door.

I leaned towards my Instant Italian book and started reading out loud: *Dov'è la stazione?? Dov'è la stazione?? Cosa fa?? Cosa fa?? Cosa fa?? Come va?? Come va?? Come va?? Va bene??*

IV   The Doors

At 5:30 p.m., 10 April 2002

I was sitting at the kitchen table having some freshly made marmalade when the doorbell rang. It was Sari, my thirteen-year-old neighbor, who together with his ten-year-old brother, Basil, managed to give me a laugh every now and then, with their hilarious videos of their karaoke competitions. In one of the films Sari appeared in his mother's dress, interrupted by a giggling Basil and the Israeli Apache helicopters in the skies of Ramallah, as well as a soldier peeing behind a tank.

"She is in the kitchen," I heard my mother-in-law tell Sari.

"Hi, Sari, have a seat. Try our marmalade, which my mother-in-law made today." I handed him a piece of bread and looked up at him. Sari, who has blond hair and a smiley thin face with round eyeglasses, looked very pale and extremely worried.

"Do you happen to have the key for Uncle Taisir's house?"

"No, why?" I asked.

"Shit, we're in big trouble. They will blow his door open, then," he said, quickly resigned to the fact.

"Are the soldiers already there?" I inquired, standing up to prepare myself.

"No, but they soon will be. They have already been to Aunt Maha's house," he replied nervously.

"I'd better move my car off the road before they smash it flat," I said. This happened to hundreds of cars parked in front of people's homes. I ran out the back door so my mother-in-law wouldn't see me, ran to the neighbors and asked them if I could park my car in their empty lot. They helped me park it.

I stood chatting with the rest of the neighbors and kids. "Three tanks and two jeeps just passed by and went up the hill," said little Sami.

"Make sure to hide your jewelry and money, put them in your bosom, *be 'Ebbech*," cried Um Sami from her balcony. "They are *haramyyeh* (thieves)—they have been stealing money mobile phones and electric gadgets, hide them all."

Oh, God damn it, Salim, how can I defend your electric gadgets? *Akeed mush bi 'ibi* (For sure, not in my bosom), I thought to myself. Every one of us, including me, was trying to hide their anxiety.

"I hope they come soon, so as to get it over with," said Abu Hasan.

"As long as they come while it's daytime, and don't get us up late at night. We'd like to sleep," added Raed with a smile.

"There is nothing to worry about. Let them come and search, we've nothing to hide," said the ice cream man.

"Did you hear? They have just arrested Naser 'Ewies, the head of Kataeb al-Aqsa," I told Raji and Raed. Breaking news, I thought.

"There will soon be a hundred Naser 'Ewieses."

Oh, well, I left it at that and went in, trying to figure out how one prepared for a house search. I watched more news on Al Jazeera.

Pretending to be calm and reasonable, I said, "Mother, it may be best to take your money and jewelry out of your bedroom. It seems there is a lot of stealing while uprooting the infrastructure of terrorism," I said.

"Why? Are they coming?" inquired Um Salim.

"No, not really, but it is always better to watch out and be prepared," I said casually.

She handed me her money and jewelry, and I put them in the big pockets of the trousers I had decided to wear before I opened the door for them. But what if I were late? They would probably detonate the front door before I got to it. I had in my mind the image of the mother and son shot dead in Bethlehem as the mother went to open the door of her veranda. Our veranda looked exactly like it. I placed the trousers on the floor next to my bed. I also got my Jordanian passport and my ID out of my purse, laid Pavarotti's CD on the living-room coffee table, took Muhammad Arkun's book *The History of Arab Islamic Thought* away from the bureau next to my bed and put the novel *Girl with a Pearl Earring* by Tracy Chevalier on top.

At around 4:30 in the afternoon the phone rang. It was Hisham, a friend of ours who works in the Ministry of Planning, inquiring whether the Israeli soldiers had reached our house, which is very close to his ministry.

"No, they have not reached us yet. I can see them near the Jawwal building, I can hear them blowing the doors off."

"But Zahi says the guards have the keys to the Jawwal building," Hisham said.

"Well, perhaps it's faster!" I said mockingly, then inquired anxiously, "Did they search Sameh's house?"

"Not yet."

"Well, it looks like both of us will have visitors tonight."

Several hours later I could still hear a few explosions up the hill from our house. I went and closed all the shutters on the northern side where the noise was coming from. I also unlocked the garden gate, and sat down at my computer to write this.

I could hear the squeaking of the tanks moving up and down the road from a distance and wondered how long it would take them to get here.

Good night.

V   Farewell, Jad

The Fourth Lifting of the Curfew
11 April 2002

I was watching the burial of the twenty-nine people killed during the first two days of the Israeli invasion of Ramallah on TV. In a mass grave, in the backyard of the hospital, twenty-nine black plastic bags were lined up with names written on each. The Israeli Army would not allow the hospital to deliver the victims to their families, nor have them buried in the town cemetery. I was mesmerized in front of the TV when my closest friend, Islah, who teaches at Birzeit University, and her eighteen-year-old daughter, Yasmin, a student there, appeared on the screen crying and sobbing hysterically like the rest of the many Ramallah residents who ran to the hospital when the curfew was lifted for the first time in six days. Sitting in front of the TV, I joined in the hysterical crying and sobbing as I wondered what brought Islah and Yasmin there. Oh, God, I hope none of Islah's relatives or friends were among the victims.

With my phone cut off, it took a few more days, until the second lifting of the curfew, before I could see Islah or talk to her.

"Well, we went to pay respects to the victims as their families could not reach them, due to the siege."

"But, Islah, why did you take Yasmin with you?" I objected.

"Yasmin and Maher (Islah's twenty-two-year-old son) went to inquire about their friend Jad."

"What about Jad?"

"Poor thing, we have no idea where he or his fellow policemen hid the night of the military invasion. Maher and I begged him to stay with us that night, but he wanted to be with his friends. Oh, God, his mother is losing her mind. She calls us every half hour from 'Azzoun (a village near Nablus)

159

asking about her son," Islah said with tears running down her cheeks.

"The first three days of the invasion, Jad was calling Maher frantically. He was seeking help and begging to be rescued. He was hiding with his friends in a building in downtown Ramallah." Both Islah and I were crying by this time.

"Believe me, Suad, Maher and I spent hours seeking help from the Red Cross and the Red Crescent. I called all international humanitarian organizations and all that we got was 'There is not much we can do, the Israeli Army is not allowing us to move. We have not been able to help the besieged or the wounded, or collect corpses from the streets of Ramallah or from inside the besieged buildings. . . .' Poor Jad, he was freaking out, and saying, 'Please help us. They are going to kill us. Please do something.' Maher was with him on the line twenty-four hours a day for three days. Then we totally lost contact with Jad. Maher and his friends think that Jad was among the fifteen hundred people arrested in Ramallah and al-Bireh. No one seems to know what happened to them.

"*Allah yesa'ed Ahelhum* (May God help their families)," she added.

"Well, Islah, take care of yourself and Maher."

I kissed her good-bye, as the three-hour lifting of the curfew was coming to an end.

I drove back home, through piles of building rubble and wreckage. As people rushed home, and Ramallah quickly turned into a ghost town again, the image of Jad's hysterical phone calls haunted me.

I cried.

It was during the fourth lifting of the curfew, a few days later, that I went to see Islah again. We were standing in front of their house with Nabil and Vanouch when Islah's oldest daughter, Sireen, came running across the street. She stood still in front of us, with tears in her eyes, and in total shock she stared at Islah. My heart sank.

"What is it?" Islah screamed. Sireen threw herself on her mother, put her arms around her and started crying.

"Jad," she said.

Islah clung to Sireen and said, "Poor thing, he knew it, my heart felt it too. Oh, God, I can't believe we have not been able to save you. . . . Please, Jad, *samehna* (forgive us). *Hazeneh emmuh* (His poor mother)," she added.

We all stood on the sidewalk crying.

"And where is Maher?" Islah asked hysterically a minute later.

"He's in the hospital," answered Sireen, wiping her tears and nose.

"Let's go and see him, Islah, he should not be left alone there," I said.

"I'm coming with you," insisted Sireen.

"*Habibti,* it may be better if you did not come," I said protectively.

"I must say farewell to Jad," she insisted.

Perhaps she's right, I thought to myself as the three of us drove towards Ramallah hospital.

"There's Maher," cried Islah.

The handsome, heavily built Maher was resisting being dragged away from the hospital by two of his friends. The minute Islah saw her son she became hysterically emotional. She opened the car door and jumped out even before I had a chance to park. Maher saw her from a distance and started crying out loud, "Mama, they killed him, they killed him, the bastards killed him, the criminals killed him, but why did they kill him? Why, Mother?"

Islah hugged Maher tightly and said, "*Ya, habibi* (my beloved), I know, *wallah* (I swear to God), I know, he was so scared I cannot believe we could not rescue him." Maher let go of his mother.

"Mama, he is wearing the green jacket and the blue shirt I gave him. They shot him in the neck here." He pointed to the back of his neck. "Mama, he has been in the hospital's morgue for thirteen days now. No one seemed to recognize him. There are three other unidentified bodies there. I saw him. I recognized his face. I kissed him good-bye. He was so cold. He was wearing the green jacket and the blue shirt I gave him," Maher repeated.

A chill ran up my whole body.

Everyone fell silent until Maher said, "Sireen, come and say farewell to Jad."

"It's OK, Maher, no need for that," I said as Sireen and Islah stood there.

"Did you call his family?" I asked, trying to distract Maher and protect Sireen from the agony.

"Yes, we called them, but they would not believe us—we had to take his photograph so we could send it to them."

Maher's two friends were standing there in silence and

total shock. They were trying to comfort Maher, but they themselves needed to be comforted.

"Mama, he was in the hospital that day when we came and asked about him, but no one seemed to have identified him."

"Come on, Maher, *habibi*. *Allah yerhamu* (God bless his soul), let's go," I said as I realized that the lifting of the curfew was about to end.

Both Islah and Sireen took Maher by the hand and got him into the car.

Islah kissed Maher's friends good-bye and we drove away in utter silence as Maher and I smoked cigarettes. A day later Maher informed me that they had succeeded in arranging for the body to be delivered to his family in 'Azzoun.

VI   Welcome Home, Salim

The Fifth Lifting of the Curfew
15 April 2002

Today is my niece Diala's birthday. She must be twenty-six this year—I'm not sure anymore. It doesn't really matter, as I cannot call her in Amman anyway.

I was delighted to hear that the curfew might be lifted today. Perhaps this would give Salim a chance to get to Ramallah from Jerusalem, where he has been trapped since he came back from France four days ago.

This time, I called Salim's cousin, Tania, to ask when she expected the curfew to be lifted.

"Vera heard from Reema, who heard from 'Abed, the baker, that they may lift the curfew from one to five this afternoon. . . . They searched Reema's house last night," Tania added.

"But I thought they had already searched her house twice?"

"Well, they came again, and wanted her to stay in the rain outside while they searched the house, but she refused, and told them she was barefooted, and a Canadian citizen. They searched the house and made a big mess of it. They also searched her car parked in the driveway. They took her flashlight, and when she complained, saying that she needed it, as the electricity was cut, they said cynically that they would bring it back in two days. 'You should be thankful we did not destroy the car,' they added. As they left, Reema wondered what else they had taken away. She was not allowed to accompany them while they entered every room. As they were leaving, she noticed that the house key was missing. She asked them if they had taken it, but they denied it."

Reema, an active member of the women's charitable organization In'ash al-Usrah, based in al-Bireh, is also a member of Birzeit University's Board of Trustees. She is seventy, a widow who lives on her own in a house close to the Palestinian Ministry of Culture, which the Israeli Army turned into a detention center when they invaded Ramallah on 29 March.

I called Salim in Jerusalem so as to coordinate with him his crossing of the two checkpoints between Ramallah and Jerusalem.

"Hello, Salim, it seems they are going to lift the curfew, so get ready to cross the al-Ram and Qalandia checkpoints, but don't bring your luggage with you. They will not let it through, and if they do, they will spend the whole day searching it, so just leave it at Reema and Alex's house."

"What about your birthday present?"

"Aah . . . my birthday present! . . ." I had totally forgotten my birthday on 12 April! "Well, it's OK, Salim, I will get it later. Just bring your identity card."

"OK, Nazmi offered to give me a ride to the Qalandia checkpoint."

"And I will pick you up at the other end."

"Can you get there?"

"Well, we'll see. I shall give it a try. Just call before you leave Jerusalem."

An hour or so later as I was sitting restlessly at home, Vera phoned. "Salim is trying to reach you. The mobile lines seem to be jammed. He says they are not allowing anyone through the Qalandia checkpoint. He does not know what to do."

"Thanks, Vera. I will call him right away."

I reached for my mobile.

"Hello, Salim."

"Yes, Suad, they have turned me back. They are not allowing anyone through the checkpoint."

"Aren't you lucky?" I said jokingly. "Well, enjoy a few more days of freedom in Jerusalem and try to come next time they lift the curfew."

I was very disappointed. I really wanted him to come back, not only because I missed him terribly, but because I was really getting claustrophobic being alone with his mother.

"No way. I shall try hard to make it, even if I have to come back to the checkpoint and try again in an hour or so."

"Good luck, Salim."

I hung up.

God, she was at it again.

"We must have lunch at one o'clock winter time, not summer time," asserted Um Salim.

"We eat when we get hungry," I said philosophically.

"I don't think we have enough left over for the three of us," she said in a worried tone.

"Don't worry, there is enough for you and Salim, as I have just eaten."

"Do you think Salim will be here by one?"

"I don't know. Let's hope so."

Twenty minutes before one o'clock, winter time, the phone rang.

"Suad, the driver says he can drive us through the dirt roads around the checkpoint."

"Salim, don't take any risks. They are crazy. They have been shooting indiscriminately."

"Well, I'm going to give it a try."

"Take care," I said as my heart sank. I really wanted him to come and take care of his mother, as I had just about had it.

"Suad, come and see if we have enough food for the three of us," she called from the kitchen.

"OK," I said in a tired voice, as if we had not been through this ten minutes before.

"Yes, Um Salim, there is plenty. Remember, I have just had a big breakfast."

"You eat at odd hours, at home. I have breakfast at eight exactly. Lunch at one, and dinner at seven exactly," she said proudly.

"Bravo, Um Salim, that's the healthy way, I know we are very disorganized."

"How come? Now that we have a curfew and you are staying home, and not working, you should be able to organize yourself a bit more."

Allahumma eytawlek ya rouh!! (Oh, God, give me patience!!)

"*SahUm Salim sah* (You are absolutely right)."

A little bit before one, the phone rang again.

"Suad, the driver is taking us through dirt roads. We are stuck somewhere close to the DCO.* We have to go back and try another road as the Israeli Army is ahead of us and we cannot advance any more."

"Salim, please, *khalas* (stop it), go back to Jerusalem," I said firmly, and I meant it, as I was getting really worried now.

"What do you mean? We cannot go back to Jerusalem now. We are very close to Ramallah."

"Then call me back when you get somewhere I can fetch you from," I said desperately.

"Are you hungry, Suad, or do you want to wait for Salim?"

"I am not hungry, I will wait for Salim."

"But I am getting hungry, it is almost one now."

"OK, why don't you eat, then?" I said impatiently.

"Which plate should I use for the microwave?"

* Israeli District Coordination Office.

The phone rang as I walked with her towards the kitchen. "Yes, Salim, where are you now?"

"The plate has to be white with no design."

"Maybe near the Jawwal building?"

"Great."

"This is way too big. Don't you have a smaller plate?"

"We are only a few minutes away from the Jalazoun Camp."

"Yes, yes, I know where you are, just stay there. I will be there in no time." I handed Um Salim the white plate with no design.

"Are you coming now?" inquired Salim as my voice disappeared while I bent down to get the plate.

"Isn't that plate too big, Suad? Don't you have something smaller?"

"No," I answered impatiently.

"You're not coming?" Salim's voice asked desperately.

"Yes, Salim. Yes, I will be there. The 'no' was for the size of the plate for your mother," I said, only adding to his confusion.

"She does not want you to come and fetch me?" he inquired in a worried voice.

"No, no. Yes, never mind. I will be there in a few minutes."

"Can you put it in the microwave for me?"

"Put more food on the plate, Um Salim, that's way too little. *Shoo had luameh bas* (Why only a tablespoonful)?"

"I want to keep the rest for Salim. Perhaps he is very hungry."

I put her plate in the microwave, waited a minute or two,

got it out of the microwave and ran out of the door to fetch Salim.

"Is it one o'clock?"

"Yes, one sharp." I banged the door behind me and dashed out with a big sigh.

As I drove up the hill, I realized I had been on this very dirt road three times in the last few days. Almost every time they lifted the curfew, I found myself on this narrow back road. The first time, I gave a ride to a person whose uncle had just been shot by the Israelis; the second time I gave a ride to two brothers whose father had died from kidney failure, as he could not reach the hospital. The third time was when I was trying hard to "get rid of" Zakiyyeh, Um Salim's helper, since having Zakiyyeh and my mother-in-law together with me at home could easily have driven me crazy—assuming I am sane now.

I found myself face-to-face with Salim carrying two bags and dragging himself up the hill. I stopped the car, jumped out and hugged and kissed him enthusiastically. Salim stood there shyly. He has never liked hugging or kissing in public.

The second we stepped into the house Um Salim said, "*Ahlan* (Welcome), my son, are you hungry?"

With great relief, I quietly withdrew into my bedroom as I heard her say: "*Fasoulia wella baitinjan mama* (Green beans or aubergine, son)?"

Later, I kissed them both good-bye, as they had decided to visit Margot, Tania and Vera. I wanted to stay home in spite of the lifting of the curfew. I did not know whether I was doing so in defiance of the Occupation or my mother-in-law. Does it really matter? I asked myself.

La Traviata loudly filled every corner of the house as I at last sat down ALONE to write.

VII   Saleh, the Blacksmith

They Lift the Curfew Once More
21 *April* 2002

I was listening to the radio as I drove to get the blacksmith to fix my mother-in-law's front door. We had been informed by Um Jamil, the only neighbor who had stayed behind in the apartment building, that the Israeli Army had blown it wide open.

Israel was refusing to receive the UN Investigation Committee in Jenin Camp.

"Israel has nothing to hide," claimed Shimon Peres.

Nevertheless, the Israeli cabinet voted unanimously against allowing the UN Commission to arrive and begin its work. Despite growing international criticism of Israel's stance, the source explained, the public relations damage being caused by the refusal was both smaller and more short term than the harm the commission could do without the safeguards and limits Israel was trying to impose on its investigation. Israel was demanding no disclosure of the witnesses' names, Israeli approval of army witnesses and immunity for its soldiers from an international tribunal. Very logical—why not? I thought to myself, as none of the "democratic and free countries" will force Israel to comply.

"It is their decision," said Kofi Annan.

I parked my car in front of the blacksmith's shop in al-Bireh.

"*Marhaba*, Saleh," I greeted him loudly.

"*Ahlan* (Welcome), Doctora Suad."

"Saleh, the Israeli Army blew open my mother-in-law's door."

"Was she hiding behind it?" he asked with a naughty laugh.

He disappeared into his workshop to gather his tools.

On our way to my mother-in-law's house, we drove along the main Nablus road. Like the rest of the town, it had become an unrecognizable war zone. My heart ached when I saw the broken trunks of the palm trees which once lined the middle island of this road.

Saleh and I chatted about the hundreds of doors he had repaired in the last few days since the Israeli withdrawal from parts of al-Bireh and Ramallah.

"I have fixed many, many doors for homes, businesses, banks, ministries, cultural centers, old people's homes and many, many clinics for many, many doctors, Doctora," Saleh told me very proudly. "They came to our neighbors' house, arrested four, but we were very lucky. They only searched our house twice. Once we were kept in one room while they searched the house, and the other time they asked us to leave the house and go down to the garden, but I was lucky, they did not arrest me."

"Ah, very lucky."

"But so what if they had arrested me; they would have let go of me in a week or ten days, like some others."

"Ya," I agreed.

171

I parked the car a few blocks from my mother-in-law's house, which is directly opposite al-Muqata'a.

"OK, let's go," I said in a confident and matter-of-fact voice.

"Ya Allah."

I got out of the car and all of a sudden it was very, very quiet, extremely quiet, abnormally quiet, as quiet as under total curfew. I started to get nervous, very nervous, extremely nervous. As Saleh opened the trunk of my car to get his tools, it all looked very suspicious to me: his big toolbag, his electrical wires, his huge cutting scissors, his long crowbar, his welding machine. Oh, my God, his welding mask looked most suspicious. Oh, no, it all looks very suspicious. How come it all looked normal and innocent ten minutes ago when Saleh put his tools in my trunk?

Come on, Suad, stop it, I thought to myself as I stared hysterically inside the trunk.

"Where is the house?" inquired the blacksmith.

"Wait, wait, Saleh, please don't get anything out of the trunk," I begged him nervously.

Saleh was looking at me inquisitively. I could see in his eyes that he was wondering, What is the matter with you, Doctora? But he said nothing; he just stared at me.

"Wait, wait, wait, Saleh, wait here, I will be back soon, let me go and check the way—the curfew, the soldiers, the tanks, whether everything is OK," I said in a panic.

"OK." Saleh stayed behind.

Nervously, I started going up the hill. Very soon I was face-to-face with a dirt mound and piles of barbed wire. Immediately behind it were four Israeli soldiers with faces painted muddy black, two on top of a tank and two in front of it. The tank was parked in front of a two-story house. The owners of this house were not as lucky as blacksmith Saleh. The owners of this house had had to totally desert it. Actually they had obviously been kicked out by the soldiers, who had camouflaged it with a big net. It looked more like a theater set than an army hideout. Why camouflage it? I thought.

Since it was dangerous to go in front of the camouflaged house, I had to go through someone's garden. "Is the curfew lifted?" I inquired.

"Yes, from ten to twelve."

"How come no one is out in the streets?" I got no answer, so I kept walking through the garden until I got to the road that led to my mother-in-law's house. Again, no one was in the streets, absolutely no one. What if they haven't lifted the curfew? I thought to myself. They will simply shoot at me. I got scared at the idea and decided to knock at somebody's door again. I saw a young and energetic woman with a striking orange dress and an even more striking bright blue headscarf cleaning her balcony.

"*Marhaba,* have they lifted the curfew?"

"From ten to twelve," she answered as she continued her impossible cleaning mission.

I kept walking straight (I think straight, but perhaps a little bit shaky), more and more nervous and more and more suspicious about my and Saleh's mission to repair my mother-in-law's door. How could I, being so nervous, convince the even more nervous and certainly more suspicious soldiers that these were really blacksmith's tools? How could I convince the soldiers before they shot at us and killed us both, or one of us, probably terrorist Saleh, that we were on a mission to repair my mother-in-law's door, the door their colleagues blew open three days previously, so that it does not remain wide open, so that their other colleagues would not be able to loot it as they had done to many, many other houses in Ramallah? It was their army's sources that admitted "ugly vandalism" against our property. Shimon Peres also said on CNN today that they were going to investigate the looting incidents in Ramallah. Well, let it be added to the long list of looting investigations.

"Hey!" I heard two of the four soldiers scream behind me. I quickly turned to face them before they shot, and screamed back, "What?" I wrung my hands together to stop the shaking. I got no answer, so I turned again and went straight to Um Jamil.

"Um Jamil, the blacksmith Saleh is here, I mean there, there in the car, but he looks, I mean his tools look, I mean he and his tools all look extremely suspicious. I brought him to fix Um Salim's door but I don't think we will fix her door today. Perhaps we'll do it when they lift the curfew another time, I mean when they leave, when they withdraw from al-Muqata'a. Never mind if they want to steal; it is OK, better than being shot, I mean better than being injured or even interrogated, or imprisoned or accused of terrorist acts. You know the tools look extremely suspicious. The mask, in particular; also, the welding machine looks exactly like Qassam 1, or is it Qassam 2? Well, you know, we really came to fix the door but it all got very complicated, very suspicious and extremely dangerous. . . ."

Um Jamil interrupted my torrent of mumblings. "Suad, what tools? What wires? What mask?"

Realizing the state I was in, Um Jamil in her very quiet and totally controlled manner said, "It's OK, Suad, some other time."

With a great sense of achievement and an even greater sense of relief, I got back to the car. "It's OK, Saleh, some other time," I said with Um Jamil's quiet confidence in my voice. I drove Saleh back to his shop. He got his tools out of my trunk. I can still recall the perplexed and puzzled expression on Saleh's face in my rearview mirror as I drove away.

14

Nablus—The Unbearable Encounter

I My Nabulsi Grandmother

We were driving on our weekly work visit to the old town of Hebron. As Farhat, Fida and Khaldun giggled in the back-seat, Nazmi complained in his usual mocking tone, "I have never met anyone who has as many grandmothers as you, Suad. How many are there? Let's count them: one from Nablus, one from Jaffa, one from Damascus, one from Hebron, one from Istanbul . . . ah . . . and . . ."

"And one from 'Arrabeh," I added proudly with a big laugh.

"Listen, Nazmi," I said playfully, "the one from Istanbul is my great-grandmother, otherwise there were only two grandmothers, one from my mother's side and one from my father's side. Both died before I was even born, but they somehow came from five or six different places, so what exactly is your problem?"

I realize this must have been a tough concept for someone

like Nazmi, whose family migrated from Hebron to Jerusalem some two hundred years ago and are still not accepted by the "original" Jerusalem families as "Jerusalemites." What is even worse is that they consider themselves "Hebronites." The problem is that Nazmi is not exactly two hundred years old, but that he acts as though he is!

"Never mind, Suad, I believe you if you insist; as a historian I have to respect people's oral tradition and history," he said in his patronizing historian voice.

"You mean fantasy history?"

"Call it what you wish."

"Then let me explain it to you," I insisted.

"No, for God's sake, don't, *wallahi*, I believe you. Anyway, it is only a two-hour drive if we are lucky with the checkpoints, your Nabulsi grandmother's stories alone need five to six checkpoints and we have only three today. Perhaps some other day."

"All right, next trip."

I heard a number of sighs of relief, some coming from behind the steering wheel, others from the backseat.

II   The Destruction of Nablus's Historic Quarter

3 April 2002

I was lying on the sofa in the living room enjoying the quiet of my mother-in-law's siesta time. I was totally drawn into Vermeer's studio, reading *Girl with a Pearl Earring*, when my eye caught the TV screen.

Once more, my heart sank as I saw the *khabar 'Ajel* (Breaking News) sign appear on Al Jazeera. With it appeared the pale and fatigued face of Walid al-Omari, Al Jazeera's main correspondent, reporting from besieged Ramallah.

"At least thirteen people from the al-Shu'bi family are feared dead under the rubble of their house in the al-Yasmineh quarter in the old town of Nablus. Their neighbors have been desperately trying to rescue them in spite of the curfew that has been imposed on the town for the last eight days."

In the same sober voice al-Omari continued: "For the eighth consecutive day, fierce fighting has taken place in the old town of Nablus. The Palestinian armed resistance has so far succeeded in stopping the Israeli Army from advancing through the narrow alleys of the town's old quarters. Many Palestinian fighters as well as civilians are feared dead. Israeli fighter planes have been bombarding the quarters of the old town. As a result many historic buildings have collapsed, among them the eighteenth-century Ottoman Caravan Sari known to locals as al-Wakalh al-Farroukiyyeh. Both the Nabulsi and Canaan soap factories have also been razed to the ground so the Israeli tanks can make their way through the narrow alleys of the old town. The Orthodox Church as well as al-Naser Mosque have been badly damaged."

"Oh, God, no!" I jumped up and screamed at the top of my voice. I hit the marble tabletop in front of me with my fist. "Oh, God, not the soap factory! When is this nightmare going to end? When will they stop destroying our historic buildings, erasing our cultural heritage?"

I started roaming nervously around the house, recalling

my last visit to the Canaan soap factory. I had watched the incredibly fascinating, rapid movements of the worker's palms as he manually wrapped the crude cubes of olive oil soap, and the up-and-down movement of the man behind him stamping on the Canaan emblem. The pouring of huge quantities of soap to form a shiny and slippery floor, the cutting of the slippery floor into small cubes and the piling of these cubes into high conical pyramids had always enchanted me.

I started thinking about how the beautifully placed pyramids of soap, which I remembered from my childhood, must have flown through the air as the F-16 airplanes hit the cross-vaulted rooms in which they were standing. The crude soap cubes, which once made the most beautiful art formations ever, and the historic stone cubes containing them were now a pile of rubble.

All of a sudden I remembered that it was the thirteen people under the rubble, all from the same family, the al-Shu'bi family, that I should have been thinking about. I was rather ashamed.

I wiped my eyes and nose on the back of my hand and went back to the sofa in the living room to watch the rest of the news.

All in all, the Israeli Army had razed to the ground 420 Palestinian villages: Saris, Bayt Jibrin, Bayt Nattif, 'Allar, Qalunya, al-Walaja, 'Emoas . . . as well as the al-Manshiyyeh neighborhood in Jaffa, the Moroccan quarter in the old city of Jerusalem, hundreds of "unlicensed" houses around East Jerusalem, dozens of houses in Khan Younis, hundreds of thousands of olive and palm trees, now the Yasmineh quarter in Nablus, and tomorrow, who knew? Perhaps the historic quarter of Hebron.

Sharon, you're bringing back our worst nightmares.

III   The Three Princesses

14 May 2002

"What got me most was the killing of a horse; the soldier opened fire at him just like that," said the taxi driver taking us to Nablus, a few days after the Israeli Army finally withdrew from the heart of the town.

"Believe me, I cried, even though it was the neighbor's horse, not mine." His voice disappeared and a few seconds later came back: "It was the first time my wife had ever seen me crying."

"Yes, I know exactly what you mean," I answered back in total sympathy, but did not dare share with him, or others in the taxi, my guilty thoughts and feelings about the destruction of historic old buildings in Nablus and the al-Shu'bi family.

"You know, I cannot get you into Nablus, but I can get you to Burin, where you can walk up the hill to the town in about thirty minutes or so."

"Of course, we know, we have been on the road, or more accurately off the road, since eight in the morning. It's already three hours now. We started our trip by walking across

Surda checkpoint mound, and then the al-Jawwal dirt mound and Dora al-Qare'. This was the worst: the Israeli Army has dug up the road and parts of the olive groves, and made a huge dirt mound at least sixty-five feet high," explained Mohannad (Riwaq's activity coordinator).

"Yes, yes, I know," answered the taxi driver.

Mohannad continued, "And there were these two little newly circumcised boys, they must have been, what, three or four years old? They were wearing their new white *jallabiyyeh* and the embroidered white-and-red head caps. Poor things— they were dragging themselves up the hill, behind their mother, as they held their *jallabiyyehs* away from their fragile bodies, just like that," demonstrated Mohannad as he pulled his shirt away from his body. Yara, Sahar, Baha and myself giggled shyly in the backseat.

The driver almost stopped the car, looked at Mohannad and said passionately, "*Uskut . . . Uskut Ya Zalameh wallah illi minshfoh min il Isrealiyyeh kull youm Jhannam* (Man . . . what the Israelis make us go through every day is worse than hell)."

It looked more like heaven to me. It was a beautiful cool and sunny spring day. I have always loved the drive between Ramallah and Nablus. I continued to drive on the old Roman road, even though most local drivers, when allowed, prefer driving on the newly constructed Jewish settlers' highway.

And now that the Israeli Army had dug up all the Palestinian roads, we were forced to drive on winding dirt paths that went through fields, hills, meadows and riverbeds.

The landscape around us looked more beautiful than ever.

I was starting to feel at one with nature as the serenity of the landscape around us seeped softly in through the back window. My eyes moved between the reddish-brown soil of the newly plowed olive terraces, the white and pink blossoms of the fruit orchards, the red poppies lining the sides of the dirt road, the gold of the vast, as yet unplowed wheat fields and the bright yellow of the wild Spanish broom under the huge oak trees.

Oh, God, it was so beautiful.

We were driving through a golden wheat field when the car suddenly got stuck.

"Get the women out of the car, and you two just push the car from behind and we will be OK." In a very matter-of-fact voice, the driver instructed the two men, Mohannad and Baha, from his seat behind the steering wheel.

"What a chauvinist driver," said Yara in a grumpy, low voice as she stepped out of the backseat of the car.

"Come on, Yara, what's the big deal? Go push the car with them if you wish," I replied. I must admit, in moments like these, I love being a woman. I pitied Mohannad and Baha. The harder the two men pushed, the more photographs we women took.

Then, like three princesses, we got back into the car. It was two in the afternoon by the time the five of us started walking up the hill for the thirty-minute walk into Nablus.

"Hurry up, we've got only two hours to see the destruction in the old town before we head back to Ramallah," said Commandante Mohannad as he led the way up the hill.

"We can always sleep in Nablus," I answered as I dragged my feet up the steep rocky path.

Mohannad stopped for a moment.

"You know something, Suad, since my son Marcel was born eight months ago, I'm scared to sleep away from home: you never know what might happen. And Fadwa does not like it either."

"Mohannad, are you, by any chance, trying to tell me that your wife still loves you?" I teased him.

"No, seriously, Suad, since I've become a father, I've somehow become a coward—I don't know how to explain it."

"Ya, ya . . . blame it on baby Marcel," said Baha.

Takh . . . takh . . . takh.

Mohannad froze and asked, "Do you hear the shooting?"

"Yes," I said shakily.

"Sure," answered Yara assertively.

"Of course," added Baha.

Some of us stood still, others were already hiding behind rocks.

"You see what I mean?" said Abu Marcel (father of Marcel) as he hid next to me. We were both kneeling behind a boulder.

The shooting continued.

I tried to hide my growing fear as the shooting got nearer and more intense.

"Well, Mohannad, what do you say? Shall we go back?" I said, my voice trembling. I was really hoping he would think about little Marcel and say yes. Perhaps that is why I asked Mohannad and not Yara, who was now leading the way up the hill.

"Come on, guys," said Yara, one of the three princesses, in her assertive voice as she kept walking steadily up the hill.

Both Mohannad and I looked at each other, seeking one another's help. We hesitantly half stood up, and with bent heads cautiously followed Yara.

"I don't think the taxi driver would be proud to see one of his two big men in hiding," said Yara to Mohannad, half joking.

Only then, with her little dig, did I realize how much Yara had taken the driver's words to heart. Mohannad ignored Yara's comment. After a few minutes he looked at me and said, "Well, my son, Marcel, is my excuse for being a coward—what is yours, Suad?"

"My little dog, Nura, but don't tell Salim," I answered with a loud laugh.

The shooting intensified.

This time, Mohannad and I hid behind two different rocks.

"Riwaq should buy its employees a good life-insurance policy before sending them out on such missions," came Baha's cynical voice from behind a third rock.

"Go back, go back, they are shooting at us," screamed a crowd of people stumbling down the hill.

"It is not only Israeli soldiers that are shooting at us, but settlers as well."

"It's the settlers that scare me most," said a young boy holding his mother's hand. "They're *weskheen* (vicious)," he added.

As more bullets flew through the skies, more people came running down the hill.

"Fuck them, this is the third day I've tried to get to the University in Nablus. I have already missed many lectures," said a young man to a friend.

"You mean to tell me al-Najah University is open?" I asked the young man hiding next to me.

"Yes, they have been teaching for three days now and I cannot get there. Every morning I try walking up different hills and different dirt paths but, *'el-'Arsat* (the fuckers) are always there and they shoot at us. The other day they shot dead a worker from Burqin as he was trying to get to his work in Nablus."

"Are you from Nablus?" asked one of the al-Najah University students.

"No, we came from Ramallah."

"Uffff . . . from Ramallah! And you are trying to get to Nablus? What for?"

"Well . . . we want to see the destruction of the historic buildings in the old town," I replied unconvincingly.

"Are you from the al-Shu'bi family? Do you know any of the people killed? Are you their friends? Seventy-six people have been killed in Nablus and *Allahu a'lam* (God knows) many more may still be under the rubble and . . . ahh . . ." he kept going.

My mobile phone rang.

"Hello, Salim, yes, we are very close to Nablus. . . . No, not in Nablus yet. . . . Yes, I know, it took us forever to get here, and now the Israeli soldiers are shooting at people trying to walk up the hill to get to Nablus. . . . Yes, yes, don't worry, your wife is certainly a coward. . . . No, no, we will definitely not take any risks. I also have four of Riwaq's employees with me and if they, *lasamahallah* (God forbid), get killed, then there will be no one left to protect the remaining historic buildings in Nablus. Well, I really want to see the destroyed buildings there. The Municipality of Nablus has already taken most of the building rubble away, as they are searching for bodies, but we've still got to see it. Don't worry, I'll call you back soon."

The two young students, as well as many others, were staring at me.

Takh takh tattatata ta ta taa.

"So, *uba'dein* (what next)?" I desperately sought Yara's advice.

"Well, let's wait. Perhaps the shooting will die down."

"Why don't we pretend we are having a picnic in the lovely olive groves?" said Baha.

We listened to Baha's advice. We sat under the olive trees, got our water out and lit our cigarettes.

We could still hear shooting in the distance.

"*Yalla,* let's go home," said Mohannad.

"It's a pity we came all the way for nothing," Yara challenged him.

"Let's wait another half hour before we give up," said Baha calmly.

"It will soon get dark, and remember, we need another three hours to get back to Ramallah," added Mohannad.

"By the way, the taxi driver said there might be another dirt road to Nablus. He can try and take us from there if we decide, but we have to decide soon as we still need to walk for a half hour or so from there," said Sahar.

"No . . . let's just quit," said Mohannad.

"No . . . let's just wait," insisted Yara.

I kept quiet, as I was getting extremely exhausted and somewhat depressed. I was really hoping they would just quit.

I did not dare express my true feelings about this trip. It would certainly be strange to admit that I never really wanted to get to Nablus. I had been dreading this trip for more than a week now. It had nothing to do with the shooting—actually the shooting gave me a good excuse to turn back.

The truth of the matter was that I was relieved the agony of this unbearable encounter was at last coming to an end.

The destruction of the old town of Nablus had filled me with the same nightmarish emotions I'd experienced during the previous two unbearable encounters of my life: my father's death, and the unfulfilled search for my family house in Jaffa.

15

Sharon and My Teflon Pan

23 September 2002

It all began in the afternoon when I was trying hard to have a siesta. On "normal" days, given the opportunity, I love to sleep at any hour of the day. This can be a source of serious tension between my insomniac husband and myself. I often jump out of bed, run to the living room sofa, sit straight and pretend to be fully awake the minute I hear Salim turning his key in the door. Salim must wonder why his wife is so slow and unresponsive after a long day of hard work.

Since 11 September, when the Israeli Army imposed a curfew on Ramallah, I had not stepped outside of our house. Last night, a bit after midnight, and for the first time in thirteen days, I stepped outside the garden gate.

Yesterday's attempt to have a siesta had nothing to do with wanting to sleep (or for that matter with Salim, who had gone abroad a few days before the imposition of this curfew); it was, rather, an unsuccessful attempt to kill a few hours of the deadly long curfew day. Perhaps being all by myself made the hours and days feel much longer.

I turned over in bed thinking of Um Salim, who once again had been trapped in her apartment. The Israeli demolition of Arafat's headquarters, using explosives, had left Um Salim alone in a house with shattered windows, a half-collapsed concrete terrace and pieces of pottery from smashed plant pots everywhere. I had not been able to reach her, as all the residential neighborhoods around the al-Muqata'a had been declared closed military areas, in addition to being under curfew. I, of course, had had difficulty trying to explain to Um Salim what it meant to be in a closed military area, in addition to being under curfew.

I forced myself to stop thinking about her, as there was nothing I could do to get her out of that area, devastated so vindictively by the Israeli Army.

I was trying hard to get some sleep, when incredibly irritating bangs came through my bedroom windows. This not-so-unrhythmic banging was much worse than the shrieking voices of the neighbor's children playing in the back garden. Often, I had to stop myself from going out and screaming my head off as they ran, shouted, fought and called on their mothers to be juries in their continual disputes. But I tell you, after thirteen days of curfew, I had decided I'd rather hear the shrieking voices of these kids than those of the screaming mothers who looked for any opportunity to take their mounting Sharonian frustrations out on their children.

The banging continued, and I found myself dashing hysterically out of the house. I found Omar, the three-year-old boy, holding a big stick and banging it, as hard as his three-year-old muscles allowed, on a Nido milk tin. I looked at him and started screaming at the top of my voice: "OMAR . . . for God's sake, stop it. Your banging is driving me crazy. *Khalas* (Enough), please." Omar looked up towards me with a pale, scared little face and a quivering lower lip, then ran complaining to his mother, leaving the stick and Nido tin behind him. Fearing that his mother might appear, I quickly sneaked back into the house.

I felt rather ashamed of myself for losing my temper at the kid, but that banging really got to me. I would have never guessed that Omar's banging would be my thirteen-day-curfew breaking point. All my attempts to have a siesta that afternoon were in vain.

I gave up, got out of bed and went back to my curfew routine:

I watched the news,

Made many cups of tea and coffee,

Checked my e-mails for the seventh time,

Visited the *Ha'aretz* Web site,

Continued reading Raja Shehadeh's book *Strangers in the House,*

Watched some more news,

Fed little Nura (I think Nura enjoys curfew days, as she gets much more than her usual one meal a day as well as spends much more time with me than usual),

Fed myself,

Stepped out of the house into the garden,

Stepped into the house again,

Talked on the phone once more; tried to analyse the political situation, asked and answered the same questions over and over again:

Would there be a war on Iraq?

Would Sharon expel Arafat this time?

Why had Sharon attacked the al-Muqata'a at this particular time? Why such an outrageous attack at this moment? Was it to prevent any anticipated reforms in the Palestinian National Authority by strengthening Arafat's international credibility and legitimacy?

The phone conversations went on and on and on for hours. Having a busy phone line only added to Um Salim's anxiety.

"I have been trying to reach you but your phone is always busy," she would often complain. "Isn't it enough that I cannot reach you or anyone else in person?"

Every time Um Salim called (and she called much more than you would think), after describing to me how these *haywanaat* (animals) had been rampaging around the al-Muqata'a, she would repeat the same question over and over again, "Suad, when do you think they're going to lift the curfew?"

"Soon, soon, Um Salim," I had repeated for thirteen days

now, with the same authoritative voice, despite not having the slightest idea if this curfew was going to be like the one imposed on Nablus some ninety-six days ago.

Being utterly bored, I went to bed relatively early. For no obvious reason, I woke up in the middle of the night. Sensing that I was awake, little Nura ran towards the door in a bid to get me to take her out for a *nunu* (pee).

Just a few minutes after I stepped back into the house, I heard lots of shooting in the distance. I carefully stepped outside again. The shooting seemed to be coming from a great distance, but the sounds were a bit strange this time. They echoed in the valleys to the west of Ramallah. Since I could not make anything out of the sounds, I walked back into the house and turned on Al Jazeera, hoping they would report something about shootings in Ramallah, but there was nothing. As the sounds came nearer and louder, I heard the neighbors saying: "Get your pots and pans out and start banging."

I ran out and saw many of the neighbors in the street.

"Pots and pans?" I inquired.

"*Tanager . . . tanager* (Pots . . . pots)!" said Sari, the neighbor's kid, laughing.

"Or have you been cooking so much that all your pots are full?" said one neighbor.

"An empty pan?" I asked, half asleep.

"A *tangarah* with *mjadara* (A pot with lentils) would also do," answered Sari with a bigger laugh.

"Or *laban emu ahsan* (cooked yogurt is better)," said Haifa.

"OK . . . OK . . . I got it," I said as I realized it was really happening and not a dream.

With great excitement I went into the house, ran to the kitchen, opened the kitchen cupboard, took out my biggest Teflon pan and came running back to the street. As I passed the living room, I glanced at the clock—it was past midnight.

Oh, God! Why do Palestinians start their civil disobedience late at night? It must be the long siestas they have been having for the last thirteen days. I went out to join the neighborhood banging crowd, only to realize I had forgotten my banging spoon. I was not suited for this kind of peaceful resistance to the Occupation, I thought to myself.

But it did not take long before I really got into it. I banged and screamed and laughed as I watched one neighbor climb on top of a roof and start banging at the metal water tank; another was banging on the electricity pole, a third on the garbage bin. It looked like a scene from a mental hospital. Never mind, I thought to myself, even if it did not send a message to Sharon and his occupying army, it was great group therapy.

I was almost breathless and totally absorbed by banging on the half-bent Teflon pan when little Omar appeared in his pink pajamas, rubbing his sleepy eyes. He came running to me and asked: "*Khalto* . . . why is banging late at night OK?"

For a second I was speechless, but soon enough I laughed and laughed, hugged little Omar tight and said: "*Habibi* Omar, I am really sorry. . . . Why don't you run now and get your Nido tin?"

Omar went back to his deserted tin pot, picked up his wooden stick and started banging with a big satisfied smile on his lovely face.

An hour or so later, when it was all over, I went back inside the house, totally exhausted.

As I was falling asleep, I wondered if little Omar was one of the young and creative new clandestine leadership of the growing Palestinian Civil Disobedience Movement!

16

A Ten-Day Relaxation Trip to Egypt

30 *September* 2003

I was crossing the Allenby Bridge with my husband and work colleagues from Riwaq. We had just come back from a wonderful and relaxing ten days away from troubled Palestine, in Cairo and Sharm esh-Sheikh.

It must have taken Mohannad at least a month of hard work to get all the necessary travel documents, permits and visas for Riwaq's twelve staff members, their spouses and children—a total of twenty-two people. Although we were "a nationally homogeneous group" (all Palestinians living under Occupation), we had at least seven different legal statuses when it came to our travel documents:

Palestinians from the West Bank with Palestinian passports

Palestinians from the West Bank with VIP diplomatic passports

Palestinians from the West Bank with Jordanian passports

Palestinians from Jerusalem (who are Israeli residents but not Israeli citizens) with Israeli travel documents

Palestinians from "1948 Israel" with Israeli passports

Palestinians from the West Bank with Canadian passports

Palestinians from the Gaza Strip living in the West Bank with Palestinian passports

The one category we did not have was Palestinians living in the Gaza Strip with Palestinian passports.

Each one of these needed a special kind of arrangement and a special kind of travel permit, not only between Ramallah–Amman–Cairo but also between Ramallah–Qalandia checkpoint–Jericho checkpoint–Jericho Resthouse (I don't know why it is called a resthouse—it is more like hell) and Allenby Bridge.

Since only two of the above seven categories were allowed to use the Tel Aviv airport, we had no option but to travel to Cairo through Amman. Most of us, but not all, needed a permit from the Jordanian Ministry of Interior to enter Jordan, even though we were technically transit passengers to Cairo.

Most of us, but not all, needed a tourist visa to Cairo. Most of us, but not all, needed a "Checkpoints Permit" from the Israeli Beit Eil headquarters near Ramallah. This kind of permit allowed one to cross some but not all of the 320 checkpoints forming the Palestinian cantons in the West Bank, but didn't allow one to enter Jerusalem or Gaza. For that you need a different kind of permit which is almost impossible to get.

Most of us, but not all, needed reservations a few months in advance on the bus which takes you from Jericho Resthouse across the river to Jordan. What would be a ten-minute drive under normal circumstances takes four to five hours. The bus reservation is needed as only three busloads a day (120 passengers) are now allowed to cross the bridge—whereas before the *intifada,** up to five thousand people a day crossed the Allenby Bridge into Jordan. Some of us, but not all, had a three-hour wait at Cairo airport before we were allowed in.

All of us, not some, had a great time in Cairo and Sharm esh-Sheikh. To be able to move about freely and stay out late at night was what we enjoyed most. We realized we had totally forgotten what *normal* life is all about.

Welcome Home

Getting to Qalandia checkpoint (which is one of the four checkpoints at the four entry points to Ramallah), we were given a warm welcome by Israeli soldiers. Because the taxi

---

* *Intifada*—the September 2000 uprising, which was a reaction to Sharon's visit to the Holy Shrine of al-Haram al-Sharif in East Jerusalem.

bringing us from Jericho was not allowed to cross the Qalandia checkpoint, we had to get out of the taxi and mount our huge amount of luggage on a *karroseh* (pedal cab). As we were doing so, we heard lots of shooting but we could not see the soldiers. "That's a nice welcome," I said. All of a sudden we saw an Israeli soldier running through the hundreds of Palestinians waiting in line to be allowed in or out of Ramallah. While he ran, the soldier pointed his machine gun in every direction. You could see dozens of Palestinians hiding behind whatever object they could find: behind cars, behind carriages in our case, and the more cautious Palestinians threw themselves on the ground. The soldier kept shooting (in the air, thank God), until he opened the door of a minibus standing across the road, grabbed a thirteen- or fourteen-year-old boy and dragged him into a small barricaded room specially installed there for "troublesome" Palestinians. We, like the rest of the Palestinians around, very quickly forgot about the boy and got back to business: bargaining with the carriage boy about the fifteen shekels (three dollars) he had asked for.

In less than a few hours, there was nothing left of our Egyptian relaxation, except for our Sharm esh-Sheikh tans.

17

A Lioness's Perspective

"Nura . . . do you want a *nunu*?"

She scampered towards the door. Half asleep, I dragged myself to open it, and she ran out into the garden. As I prepared my two huge mugs of tea with milk I heard a gunshot from the Surda checkpoint less than a half mile away. Carrying my mugs, I went back to bed. Nura had also made it back to her bed, next to ours, but neither Salim nor Nura get cups of tea. Salim was listening to the news with his eyes shut.

I tiptoed around, choosing my clothes. I needed an elegant outfit that morning, as I was going to be on American television, in a desperate attempt to convince the viewers of Bob Simon's CBS program *60 Minutes* of the terrible impact of the Separation Wall* on our lives.

Later, I drove my car on a dirt road, followed by the CBS

---

* The Separation Wall is a twenty-six-foot-high concrete wall in some areas, and in others an electrified wire fence. The 430-mile-long wall was approved by the Israeli security cabinet in August 2002, ostensibly to prevent Palestinians from

crew. I stood against the Rafat fence, which prevented me and other colleagues at Riwaq from reaching our conservation projects outside Ramallah.

"*No,* this stupid wall has nothing to do with Israel's security. Look at it. It does not separate Israel from Palestine, it separates Palestinians from Palestine. This wall, like the majority of the three hundred and twenty checkpoints, has *nothing* to do with Israel's security! If Israel wants a security separation wall, it must build the wall and the checkpoints on the 1967 borders, not inside our land. This is the biggest land and water *grab* in the history of Israel. While claiming to separate themselves from us, they have taken up to fifty-five percent of our land. Do you call this security?" I found myself screaming at Bob Simon. I think he regretted choosing a middle-aged, menopausal woman to talk about *separation*.

That afternoon I had an even longer siesta. It was so long, I woke up on Monday morning.

Monday, 27 October

"Nura . . . *nunu?*"

Ran towards the door, half awake, opened the door, ran

---

entering Israel. Only 11 percent of the wall follows the 1967 borders. The wall disturbs the lives of 680,000 Palestinians and has resulted in massive land confiscations, the dismemberment of farming communities and so far the uprooting of around 1.2 million olive trees (amounting to 10 percent of all olive trees in the West Bank). One hundred twenty-five miles of the wall have so far been constructed. On 9 July 2004, the International Court of Justice at The Hague decided that the wall is illegal and should be dismantled. Israel vows to continue its construction.

to the garden, two huge mugs of tea with milk. I heard an Israeli helicopter roaming in the sky of Ramallah; carried my two mugs to bed, Nura back to her bed, Salim listening to the news:

"The American administration is critical about Israel's construction of the Security Wall inside the Palestinian Territories, hence depriving Palestinians from reaching their farms."

Had my interview with Bob Simon (which had not been transmitted yet) already influenced the American administration?

Tuesday, 28 October

I was trying hard to hide my anxiety and fear from Leila Shahid, the Palestinian ambassador in Paris, whom I was accompanying on her trip to the town of Qalqiliah, some thirty-one miles north of Ramallah. She wanted to see the worst of the Separation Wall.

The problem was not the three types of permits I needed to "legally" accompany Leila on her trip, or the impossibility of getting such permits from the Israeli Army at such short notice, but rather the mental and psychological barriers, checkpoints and separation walls I had personally built in and around myself and my life, in besieged Ramallah. I must admit I was in a state of complete denial about the harsh realities of Qalqiliah's twenty-six-foot-high concrete wall. Denial seemed to me an effective way of dealing with the unbearable encounters of life under occupation.

To drive "illegally" through Israel seemed to be the only way to make it to Qalqiliah. It was also the only way to challenge Sharon's "Security Wall"!

It was my *age* that got us through the Qalandia checkpoint, Leila's *elegance* through the second checkpoint into Israel and the soldiers' total *confusion* over Leila's passport and my Jordanian passport that got us through the *only* entry and exit point for the 45,000 residents of Qalqiliah. We later learned that we were lucky to get through, as the gate had been closed by the Israeli Army for the last twelve consecutive days.

"*Erghjaa la wargha* (Back up)!" the soldiers kept yelling at us and all others trying to get into town.

"Back where?" Leila and I inquired.

"Don't listen to him, he is stupid, all he wants is to give orders, and his orders are even more stupid," said an elderly woman standing just behind us.

We take orders only from older women, so we just continued our conversation.

"Are you from Qalqiliah?" Leila asked the three young women standing next to her.

"Yes, we're from Qalqiliah, but we teach in the girls' school in the neighboring village of Jayyous."

" *'Azab* (It's a hassle)," said her friend, "going and coming, we have to cross this checkpoint and another checkpoint in Jayyous. We have to take four taxis, and walk up and down mounds of rubble in order to reach our students—*moush 'eisheh* (it's not a life)."

"And most of the time the checkpoint is closed," said a third teacher to Leila.

202

Leila listened attentively to the three teachers. I watched the long queue of women on the other side of the checkpoint. The only Arab tradition the Israeli soldiers seem to reinforce, while still humiliating every man and woman, is gender separation.

As two Israeli female soldiers body-searched each one of the women, my eyes moved from one face to the other. I felt myself absorbing the feelings expressed on the faces of these women the second they were touched by the soldier: anger, frustration, weariness, pity, helplessness, humiliation, defiance, disgust and resentment.

I was enraged.

"Look, there is a male soldier searching the poor women, unbelievable," said Leila.

"No, Loulou, these are women soldiers."

"Really?"

I guess once you are a soldier all gender differences disappear.

"Come forward," the same stupid soldier called us.

The three teachers went first, Leila second and I followed.

Leila and I were met by Abu Ma'zoz, an official from the Municipality of Qalqiliah. Abu Ma'zoz realized that Leila and I had come to see the Separation Wall, so immediately after greeting us he said, "You see, we are like a Coca-Cola bottle with a cap. The Israeli Army has barricaded or closed all other entrances to Qalqiliah." I wondered if this was a good ad for Coca-Cola.

Abu Ma'zoz started familiarizing us with our surroundings. He pointed east: "You see the Jewish settlement over there? That's Egal Alef and next to it is Egal Beit. The one straight ahead is Sufein. It was Sufein's settlers who stole our *jarrafeh* (Caterpillar), but we managed to get it back."

I wanted to stop Abu Ma'zoz and ask him how one can steal a caterpillar. But then I felt embarrassed to see all the stolen land in front of my eyes and inquire only about the *jarrafeh*. I stopped myself from asking and continued listening to Abu Ma'zoz: "See that huge settlement over there, to the south? That is Alfeh Manasheh."

We drove along the Nablus road, Qalqiliah's main shopping street. Having very few people in the street compelled me to inquire if the town was under curfew.

"No, it is Ramadan and since the checkpoint has been closed for twelve consecutive days, people have stopped venturing in or out of Qalqiliah," said Abu Ma'zoz.

Leila and I were driven alongside the wall, which totally surrounds Qalqiliah. We learned that 45 percent of the town's land and nineteen of its wells are now out of reach, i.e., on the "other side" of the wall. To get to their agricultural fields, villagers had to pass through the one entry/exit to their town. Even though it was the end of October, villagers had not been permitted to harvest their olives yet.

A seventy-year-old farmer, Abu Mohammad, stood next to the twenty-six-foot, brutal concrete wall. He was wearing the biggest square spectacles ever. "I am replacing the olive, palm and fig trees which were uprooted by the Israelis to build this wall." Abu Mohammad pointed towards the wall, then bent over and continued digging. At that very moment I wondered whether Abu Mohammad would live long enough to see these slow-growing trees blossom. I wished I had the same-sized glasses (but dark ones) to hide my tears from Abu Mohammad's wrinkled face. As Leila and I walked away from the wall I heard Abu Mohammad say, "This is the third time I've started all over again."

The tears running down my face stopped me from going back and listening to what else he wanted to say.

Wednesday, 29 October

"Yes, we'd love to visit the zoo," both Leila and I answered enthusiastically.

We knew that Qalqiliah's municipality was politically progressive and had many pioneering projects. The Arab mayor of Qalqiliah and the Meritz mayor of the neighboring Israeli town of Kfar Saba had twinned the two towns, and the progressive Israelis in Kfar Saba had petitioned Sharon's government, asking it to take Jewish land for the construction of the wall. But a zoo! That was really a pioneering project—there was no other zoo in the West Bank or Gaza Strip.

Our tour of the zoo started with the delightful baby giraffe, which had been shipped all the way from South Africa. I wondered if this was a present from the ANC to the Palestinian people. Unlike the rest of the animals in Qalqiliah's zoo, the baby giraffe seemed to be totally ambivalent about the political situation, perhaps because she could see behind the wall.

Next to the giraffe, on a concrete platform in the middle

of a tiny barbed-wire cage, sat the proud elderly lioness. We were discreetly informed that she had recently lost her beloved husband. The minute I got close to the lioness and before I could even utter my condolences, she looked me straight in the eyes and said, "Now you know what it means to be living in a cage, isolated and cut off from your natural habitat."

"I know, I am really sorry, we owe you an apology."

"It's OK, it is the Israelis that owe us both many apologies," added the lioness.

We hugged one another and cried.

Having nothing else to tell the lioness, I walked away towards the monkeys' cage.

At first, the almost thirty monkeys stood still and looked as depressed as the lioness and the rest of us living under occupation. But not having seen any visitors in months, they soon got excited and started showing off: some hung from their hands, others from their tails; a few swung from their legs, and some bounced between the four walls of their cage. It was so touching I cried. Behind us appeared Said, the keeper, carrying two huge buckets of persimmon fruits. He opened the cage door and started throwing in the delicious big persimmons. Soon the cage floor had a fluffy orange carpet.

"As the farmers of Qalqiliah are unable to sell their fruit and vegetables in the markets beyond the wall and the checkpoint, we feed it to the monkeys," he said.

By the time Said had finished explaining, each monkey had five to six persimmons in its lap, and was pushing another two or three into its mouth.

I liked the monkey spirit.

I took a persimmon and joined in.

Thursday, 31 October

A severe pain in my stomach woke me up early. I took Nura out for a *nunu*. With no mugs of tea, I went back to bed.

I could not quite tell whether it was the image of the high concrete wall, or the image of Abu Mohammad planting olive trees against the wall, or the deathly sad look of the lioness in the zoo, or the Palestinian being beaten up in the military cage at the Qalandia checkpoint or the tears quietly running down Leila's cheeks as we drove back that caused my stomachache to continue for the whole of Thursday.

Of course, the Israeli planes roaming the skies of Ramallah for hours on end did not help.

As I lay there, I recalled what Ariel Sharon had said in 1973, when asked by Winston S. Churchill III, grandson of the former British prime minister, how Israel would deal with the Palestinians: "We'll make a pastrami sandwich of them. We'll insert a strip of Jewish settlements in between the Palestinians, and then another strip of Jewish settlements right across the West Bank, so that in twenty-five years, neither the United Nations, nor the U.S.A., nobody, will be able to tear it apart" (*Water and Land Grab Report 2003*).

It had taken Sharon an extra five years to make a concrete wrapper around the pastrami sandwich.

BAGHDAD DIARIES
by Nuha al-Radi

In this moving account of life in Baghdad during the first war on Iraq and in virtual exile in the years following, Iraqi artist Nuha al-Radi immerses us in the day-to-day reality of life lived in wartime. We get to know her family and friends, and witness first-hand the effects of bombing and embargoes on ordinary people. But what emanates most vibrantly from these diaries is the spirit of endurance and the celebration of the smallest of life's joys.

Memoir/Current Affairs • 1-4000-7525-4

SEARCHING FOR HASSAN
by Terence Ward

Growing up in Tehran in the 1960s, Terence Ward and his brothers were watched over by Hassan, the family's cook, housekeeper, and cultural guide. Forty years later, Ward embarked on a pilgrimage with his family in search of Hassan. Across the landscape of Iran, he plumbs its rich past, explores its deep conflicts with its Arab neighbors, and anticipates the new "Great Game" now being played out in central Asia. Insightful and moving, *Searching for Hassan* enhances our understanding of the Middle East with the story of a family who came to love Iran through their affection for its people.

Memoir/Current Affairs • 1-4000-3223-7

I SAW RAMALLAH
by Mourid Barghouti

Barred from his homeland after 1967's Six-Day War, Mourid Barghouti spent thirty years in exile—shuttling among the world's cities, separated from his family, never certain whether he was a visitor, a refugee, a citizen, or a guest. As he returns home for the first time since the Israeli occupation, he crosses into Ramallah and is unable to recognize the city of his youth. Sifting through memories of the old Palestine, he discovers what it means to be deprived of "the habitual place and status of a person." *I Saw Ramallah* is a deeply humane book, essential to any balanced understanding of today's Middle East.

Middle Eastern Studies/Memoir • 1-4000-3266-0

MEZZATERRA
by Ahdaf Soueif

From the author of *The Map of Love*, an incisive collection of essays on Arab identity, art, and politics that seeks to locate the mezzaterra, or common ground, in an increasingly globalized world. The criticism and commentary collected here have earned Ahdaf Soueif a place among our most prominent Arab intellectuals. Clear-eyed and passionate, they are the direct result of Soueif's own circumstances of being "like hundreds of thousands of others: people with an Arab or a Muslim background doing daily double-takes when faced with their reflection in a Western mirror." Soueif's deeply intelligent, fearless essays embody the modern search for identity and community.

Essays/Current Affairs • 1-4000-9663-4

OUT OF PLACE
by Edward W. Said

A fatal medical diagnosis convinced Edward Said to leave a record of where he was born and spent his childhood; with this memoir he rediscovers the lost Arab world of his early years in Palestine, Lebanon, and Egypt. Said writes about his birthplace in Jerusalem, schools in Cairo, and summers in the mountains above Beirut, revealing an unimaginable world of rich, colorful characters and exotic Eastern landscapes. Underscoring all is the confusion of identity the young Said experienced as he came to terms with the dissonance of being an American citizen, a Christian and a Palestinian, and, ultimately, an outsider.

Memoir • 0-679-73067-2

THE STORYTELLER'S DAUGHTER
by Saira Shah

As an accomplished journalist and documentarian, Shah returned to her exiled family's homeland cloaked in the burqa to witness the shocking realities of Afghan life. As the daughter of the Sufi fabulist Idries Shah, primed by a lifetime of listening to her father's stories, she eagerly sought out, from the mouths of Afghan refugees in Pakistan, the myths that still sustain this battered culture of warriors. And she discovered that in Afghanistan all the storytellers have been men—until now.

Memoir/Middle Eastern Studies • 1-4000-3147-4

VINTAGE BOOKS • ANCHOR BOOKS
Available at your local bookstore, or call toll-free to order:
1-800-793-2665 (credit cards only).